CW00923323

Sheltered and Retirement Housing: A Good Practice Guide

Imogen Parry and Lyn Thompson

Chartered Institute of Housing

The Chartered Institute of Housing
The Chartered Institute of Housing is the professional organisation for people who work in housing. Its purpose is to maximise the contribution housing professionals make to the wellbeing of communities. The Chartered Institute has over 19,000 members across the UK and the Asian Pacific working in a range of organisations, including housing associations, local authorities, the private sector and educational institutions.

Chartered Institute of Housing
Octavia House, Westwood Way
Coventry CV4 8JP
Tel: 024 7685 1700 Fax: 024 7669 5110
Website: www.cih.org

Sheltered and Retirement Housing: A Good Practice Guide
Imogen Parry and Lyn Thompson
Editor: Jane Allanson

1 903208 94 7

Layout by Jeremy Spencer
Cover illustration by Sandra Howgate
Printed by Genesis Print and Marketing

Contents

Foreword

THE NATURAL CHOICE
FOR A HAPPY RETIREMENT

McCarthy & Stone is the UK's leading provider of private sheltered housing. With over 600 developments around the country we have provided about 30,000 new, purpose built homes for older owner-occupiers in the last 20 years.

Looking forward, I believe that sheltered housing will make a major contribution towards improving choice and independence for older people in our society. Sheltered housing provides residents with the security they so desperately want, accessibility, companionship and the mutual support required to cope with challenges of old age. It is hard for people who have not visited a sheltered housing development to appreciate how much residents gain from, and give back to, their local communities once they are freed from the worries and pressures of living alone and maintaining their traditional family house.

Only by understanding our customers and responding effectively to their needs can my company's business continue to grow successfully. This may sound obvious, but McCarthy & Stone is often in a position of having to remind others of the merits of sheltered housing, why people choose to live there and how it can positively change their lives. In 2003 we commissioned independent research which demonstrated how moving into private sheltered housing had significant effects on residents' quality of life, health and general sense of wellbeing. The research found, for example, that 64% of residents felt their wellbeing had improved since moving in and 83% said it had helped maintain their independence. Notwithstanding an average age of over 79 years, 41% reported that their health had improved. A huge 92% would recommend sheltered housing and their way of life to their friends!

We must not ignore, however, the crucial elements behind successful sheltered housing. Sensitive and effective management of schemes is what underpins a positive atmosphere in a development. For developers like McCarthy & Stone, quality in the design and, above all, appropriate location are absolutely essential to attract customers and ensure a scheme's long term success. That said, both public and private sectors still have much to do in convincing some housing authorities, social services and the Government of the beneficial role sheltered housing can play in giving the increasing numbers of older people a better quality of life.

McCarthy & Stone is delighted to be sponsoring this Guide and, as a CIH member, I would like to thank the Institute for all they are doing to improve housing choice for older people. I trust that readers of the Guide will find it both interesting and informative.

Gary N Day MRTPI, ACIH
Land and Planning Director
McCarthy & Stone plc

ADDITIONAL SPONSORS

StepForward

StepForward, a member of Metropolitan Housing Partnership, is a specialist social care and support provider dedicated to enhancing the lives of people with a wide range of needs. With bases in London and the Midlands, we provide support to nearly 3,000 people across 16 Supporting People Administering Authorities. Together with Metropolitan Housing Trust we have over 30 years experience of providing a range of sheltered housing and extra-care services designed to enable people to maximise independence, increase access to services and enhance quality of life. StepForward is a member of ERoSH and actively supports the sharing of good practice across the sheltered housing sector.

Sanctuary Housing

With over 35 years experience, **Sanctuary** is one of the UK's leading Housing Associations employing more than 2,400 people nationwide with over 41,000 properties in management in the UK. Sanctuary's core business is providing accommodation of different types including houses for rent or sale, shared ownership, sheltered housing and homes for those with special needs. As a not for profit organisation, our income is used for updating and developing our services and maintaining our properties to high standards. Sanctuary is a fast growing organisation and, in addition to providing social housing, has diversified into the commercial areas of Care and Management Services.

HANOVER

Founded in 1963, **Hanover** was the first national housing association building for older people. With over 17,000 properties across 400 estates, today we are one of the leading housing and support providers for older people in England.
We are driven by our vision of "a society in which older and disabled people can freely choose and afford the housing and support options that suit them best."
Although sheltered housing makes up the bulk of the property we manage, Hanover has also been a leading proponent of the extra care housing model for frailer older people. We are pleased to see how our original model has grown and diversified, and has become widely adopted as a positive housing and care choice.
We have one of the largest portfolios of ExtraCare housing, with 40 estates in management throughout England.

ACKNOWLEDGEMENTS

The Chartered Institute of Housing would like to thank McCarthy & Stone for providing sponsorship to fund this publication, and to thank Gary Day, Land and Planning Director at McCarthy & Stone, for his support and interest in the project.

Thanks and appreciation are also extended to Hanover Housing Association, Sanctuary Housing Association and StepForward (part of Metropolitan Housing Partnership) for sponsoring and supporting the Guide.

The authors and publishers are indebted to the many organisations which provided good practice examples. Many more examples were received than space permitted to include in the Guide.

Many people generously gave their time to read and comment on drafts of the Guide or to help shape parts of it. Their help is greatly appreciated, and they include Jim Anderson (Castlehill HA), Nigel Appleton (consultant), Pat Black (Sanctuary HA), Moya Cherrington-Day (Southern Housing Group), Stephen Clarke (ODPM), Kathy Davidson (Aberdeenshire Council), Jackie Dix (Age Concern Cymru), John Galvin (Elderly Accommodation Counsel), Cynthia Gibbs (Peverel), Denise Gillie and Paul Watson (both then at Dept of Health), Domini Gunn-Peim (Audit Commission), Helena Herklots (Age Concern), Andrew Kean (ODPM), Bronwen Lloyd (Charter HA), Peter Lloyd (University of Sussex), Darshan Matharoo (Beth Johnson Housing Group), John Mills (ARHM), Angela Mkandla (Leeds City Council), Kate Oldfield (Sanctuary HA), Steve Ongeri (Housing Corporation), Sue Parslow (Home Housing Group), Meic Phillips (Epic Trust), Jeremy Porteus (Dept of Health), Steve Rafferty (independent trainer), Melanie Rees (Audit Commission), David Smith (Atlantic Housing Group), Graeme Watson (Tenants First).

Several CIH staff contributed to the progress of the Guide, including Debbie Larner, Marion Conlon, Niki Walton, Marie Vernon, Jenny Mills, Alison Roberts, Lyn Jardine and Sarah Davis.

In researching and writing the Guide, the authors drew on their extensive experience of working with many people involved in sheltered housing - from scheme managers to directors and tenants - and they thank all these individuals whose ideas and commitment have influenced their thinking.

About the Authors

Imogen Parry

Imogen Parry has specialised in training, policy and strategy relating to older people's housing for over 18 years. She moved from social work to lecturing in social policy in the late 1970s and, with Lyn Thompson, developed one of the first National Warden Certificate Courses, at the College of North East London, in 1987. Following the publication in 1993 of the first edition of *Effective Sheltered Housing* (co-authored with Lyn) Imogen joined Sanctuary Housing Association in 1994 as Senior Policy Manager (Older People). At Sanctuary, Imogen led two sheltered housing service reviews, the programme of remodelling sheltered stock, the writing of the sheltered scheme manager's manual, a review of out of hours services and the development of a diversity strategy for sheltered housing. Since leaving Sanctuary in early 2003 Imogen has worked as a freelance consultant and trainer, working alone and with other consultancies, specialising in strategic reviews of sheltered housing, developing sheltered housing policies, the quality requirements of Supporting People, tenant consultation and adult protection policies and training. Imogen was a founder member of ERoSH, the national charity promoting sheltered housing, and is a trustee and member of its collaboration and development group. Imogen continues to contribute to conferences and journals on the role and future of sheltered housing. She can be contacted via email: imogen.parry@btopenworld.com

Lyn Thompson

Lyn has been committed to the development of the sheltered housing service and its staff since 1978, as a practitioner in local authorities and housing associations, as a teacher and trainer, and through her writing and consultancy activities. Lyn has been joint author of all three CIH sheltered housing guides, the first of which was written with Imogen Parry when both were teaching sheltered housing staff at the College of North East London (CONEL). Lyn left her post as Head of Housing Studies at CONEL to join the Centre for Sheltered Housing Studies (CSHS) in 1997, where she was initially responsible for the development of learning materials and the delivery of a range of courses for those working in sheltered housing. More recently her role has been concerned with the management of a European-funded EQUAL action research project, 'Lifelong Learning/Active Ageing', based in seven sheltered housing settings across the UK. In addition, Lyn has been closely involved with the development of the CSHS Code of Practice for Sheltered Housing. These initiatives promote quality of service and quality of life within sheltered housing, two key objectives to which Lyn has been committed since 1978, and which she will continue to take forward on leaving CSHS at the end of June 2005. Lyn plans to join her husband's training and consultancy service, where she can be emailed at: pgriseri.associates@virgin.net

Introduction

This is a time of unprecedented change in the field of housing for older people. Service providers are facing new challenges in terms of the social and regulatory environment within which they operate. A growing and increasingly diverse generation of older people is seeking accommodation which meets a wide range of needs and expectations. Rented sheltered housing is in the spotlight, subject to external scrutiny for the first time, with service users widely encouraged to exercise choice and control. Older owner occupiers have a range of choices open to them, including, for leaseholders, the right to take over the management of their properties.

It has never been more important for sheltered and retirement housing to be delivered and managed effectively and to be an integral part of the local strategy for older people's services, and this Guide looks at how to achieve these aims. While many of the topics covered are relevant to both sheltered and retirement housing, the Guide is essentially aimed at sheltered housing for rent and looks at the current changes taking place in the sector. Within this book, the term 'retirement housing' is used to describe leasehold housing schemes which meet the needs of older owner-occupiers.

Some shining examples of excellent, innovative, customer-focused practice can be found within the UK's 600,000 units of rented sheltered housing, managed by large and small, specialist and non-specialist, local authority and housing association providers. However, there is also a legacy of mediocre, poor or sub-standard provision, to which providers are now giving their attention, aware of the need to offer accommodation and support that meets the changing expectations of current and future generations of service users.

Supporting People, Best Value and their associated inspection and monitoring regimes have acted as a huge catalyst for change. Inspection and review outcomes have identified much that is positive and innovative within older people's housing services. Older people have expressed their satisfaction with living in easy-to-manage accommodation, with support when needed, and good practice and positive findings have been widely shared across the sector.

Despite this, however, as out-of-date services have been exposed through the inspection and review processes, there seems to be a growing, anecdotally based belief that much sheltered housing is "past its sell-by date", to quote one Supporting People Lead Officer. Such negative views of sheltered housing can be found within inspection reports, expressed at conferences, and within the housing and social care press.

These negative perceptions, based on knowledge of the poorest provision or on a lack of wider awareness, should not be allowed to undermine the whole sector, and in particular the hard work that most providers are currently undertaking to significantly improve their services and ensure their strategic relevance to older people's services. The table below illustrates some of the criticisms, often outdated, made of sheltered and retirement housing, with the right hand column showing the corresponding initiatives and good practice which the best providers are already achieving, and which many others are actively working towards in order to ensure their provision meets the needs of the next generation of older people.

Contrasting views and perceptions of sheltered and retirement housing

Typical criticisms	The wider picture
"Sheltered and retirement housing consists of unattractive, small and hard-to-let properties, frequently bedsits"	• Sheltered and retirement housing aims to offer compact and easily managed accommodation • Scheme reviews have identified hard-to-let properties or those needing refurbishment • Action plans are in place to implement necessary changes (which could include refurbishment to provide Extra Care housing, or the provision of Intermediate Care beds)
"Sheltered and retirement housing schemes are 'ageist ghettoes' in which older people are isolated from the wider community"	Sheltered and retirement housing offers older people the choice of living together in communities, where: • There are a range of opportunities for interaction with the wider community • Residents' views are sought and acted upon • A range of opportunities exist for participation and empowerment →

Typical criticisms	The wider picture
"The warden's role is unclear; they are an isolated workforce, not recognised by other professionals (health, social services); their residential status creates problems both with recruitment and in terms of the Working Time Directive"	Scheme managers are well-trained professionals who: • Work a 9-5 day • Do not necessarily live at the scheme • Are line-managed by knowledgeable staff • Work collaboratively with colleagues in other agencies to provide a 'seamless service' to residents
"Sheltered housing does not offer value for money"	Sheltered housing schemes are a community resource in terms of: • The building, where those living outside the scheme are welcome to attend a range of activities • The scheme manager, who offers advice, advocacy and support to older people living in their individual homes within the wider local community • All rented schemes are preparing for reviews and inspections in which the value for money they offer will play a key part • On average, the support costs within sheltered housing are very low per tenant per week compared with other forms of supported housing
"Providing sheltered and retirement housing puts pressure on public resources"	Living in good quality sheltered and retirement housing contributes to older residents' health and wellbeing, resulting in fewer demands on health and social care services
"Sheltered and retirement housing does not meet the wide range of needs represented by the UK's increasingly ageing and increasingly culturally and ethnically diverse older population"	Sheltered and retirement housing providers are planning and developing new and re-modelled provision which is designed to meet the needs of an increasingly diverse older population

Groups such as ERoSH, and initiatives such as the CSHS Code of Practice for Sheltered Housing, have led the way in recent years by aiming to ensure good practice becomes common practice, through raising awareness and encouraging and supporting sheltered and retirement housing providers to commit to quality and to publicise and share excellence.

More recently, preparation for the Supporting People programme has motivated many more providers to review and improve services. Whatever stage providers have reached on their journey towards excellence, the focus on continuous improvement within the current inspection regimes and quality initiatives means that no-one can stand still. However good their practice is, they must seek to get better. There are many examples, reflected within the case studies in this book, which show how a diverse range of providers are at different stages within the 'reinvention' process, addressing key aspects of service provision and delivery in imaginative and flexible ways.

The view that sheltered housing is obsolete is firmly challenged by the excellent practice, commitment to quality and innovative ideas which can be seen in much sheltered housing across the UK which clearly meets the current and future needs of older people. Given the right leadership and clear goals, sheltered housing can respond to changing environments and reinvent itself, and indeed in many cases it already has.

This Guide aims to help providers with this process, whatever stage they have currently reached. It is intended primarily for sheltered and retirement housing staff working at front line, service management and director levels. However, it will also be a resource for other professionals such as members of Supporting People teams and other staff involved in service reviews and inspections, and for health and social services authorities, key partners in the reinvention of sheltered housing now taking place.

While the discussion of performance and regulatory requirements and funding regimes focuses on the specific framework in England, the key themes of the Guide are relevant throughout the UK. The terminology and agencies discussed refer to the experience in England, and the authors and publishers acknowledge that variations exist in other countries in the UK.

The examples of good practice and innovation which appear throughout the book transcend the type, size and location of the provider. These case studies show good practice and positive outcomes which can be achieved by all. They are intended to inspire everyone involved in the commissioning, provision, management and delivery of housing and support services to older people, and to assist in the shared quest to ensure a robust, flexible and user-focused service which will remain within its sell-by date for many years to come.

Chapter 1 outlines the changing context within which sheltered and retirement housing now operates. In the rest of the Guide the various strands of these changes are addressed in more detail:

- Chapter 2 explores the changing role of the scheme manager
- Chapter 3 considers the implications of working with an increasingly diverse range of service users
- Chapter 4 emphasises the need for effective partnership working
- Chapter 5 sets out the new regulatory and contract framework within which sheltered housing operates
- Chapter 6 sets out good practice for strategic management of the service

Finally, in Chapter 7, the Guide draws together a range of key issues which sheltered housing providers must consider in order to prepare their service for the challenges of the future.

CHAPTER 1

THE CHANGING CONTEXT

This chapter outlines the rapidly changing context for sheltered and retirement housing. It considers the key drivers for change and the factors that will influence the planning, provision and management of sheltered housing over the next five to ten years including:

- Demographic trends
- Changing expectations
- Issues of tenure
- Key strategies influencing sheltered and retirement housing
- Supporting People
- The continuum of care and support for older people.

❑ 1.1 Demographic trends affecting sheltered and retirement housing

In the United Kingdom, in 2002, according to estimates based on the 2001 Census of Population, there were over 10.9 million people of pensionable age:

- 9,101,000 in England
- 950,000 in Scotland
- 588,000 in Wales
- 266,000 in Northern Ireland.

Of the total numbers of older people in the UK, in 2002:

- 4,464,000 were aged 75 and over
- 1,124,000 were aged 85 and over.

This represents an increase from the previous census, and the older population of the UK continues to rise. Further trends from the 2001 census with implications for sheltered and retirement housing providers include:

- Increased life expectancy, based on improved health care and living standards, has resulted in the ageing of the population of the UK as a whole; for the first time, the number of those aged over 60 is greater than the number of under-16s.
- The proportion of older black and minority ethnic (BME) people can also be expected to increase. For example, the 2001 census showed that 9% of Black Caribbeans, and between 2% and 6% of other BME groups, were aged over 65. Chapter 3 of this Guide looks at how providers can best ensure their services meet the diverse social, religious and cultural needs of these groups.
- An increase in numbers of the very old (aged over 85) which has clear implications for sheltered and retirement housing housing providers:
  - In 2001 4% of people aged 65-69, 7% of people aged 70-74, 10% of people aged 75-79, 13% of people aged 80-84 and 19% of people aged 85 and over lived in sheltered accommodation.
  - As people age in place within sheltered housing, and as the age of those moving into sheltered housing increases, the need for appropriate support and care provision rises correspondingly.
  - In particular, the numbers of mentally frail older people are increasing as people live longer. The Alzheimer's Society estimates that there are currently over 750,000 people in the UK with dementia, of which the majority (97.5%) are aged over 65. The chances of having the condition rise with age: 1 in 20 people aged 65 and over, and 1 in 5 people aged 80 and over, will develop dementia.

In the early days of sheltered housing it was envisaged that, as people became older and frailer, and their physical and mental health deteriorated, they would make a further move into residential care. However, residential care provision itself has reduced in recent years, and the concept of 'moving on' is now outdated. Most sheltered housing providers now aim to provide service users with a home for life, supported by care packages delivered, generally through a joint working or partnership arrangement, to people in their homes. This in turn presents a challenge to providers – how best to give support to very frail or dependent older people, in particular those with dementia?

The issues and implications arising from these demographic trends are considered further throughout this Guide.

❑ 1.2 Changing expectations

Changes in older people's expectations have had a widespread impact on sheltered and retirement housing providers. Potential residents are put off by unsuitable buildings, inconvenient locations and the outdated culture of a 'warden' service.

Many providers have begun to respond to the higher aspirations of the current 'younger generation' of older people, and to anticipate what future customers are likely to demand.

Out-of-date buildings may still feature bedsits and shared bathrooms, or lack other facilities or simply have an old-fashioned, ethnocentric and institutional appearance, and frequently fail to meet the Decent Homes Standard. In response, many providers have undertaken remodelling programmes, although generating funding for such initiatives can present problems. ALMO funding, for example, only enables providers to bring their housing up to the Decent Homes Standard, and does not cover the full remodelling that is often required to bring the scheme up to a level that will be acceptable to older people in the future.

Some providers have remodelled hard-to-let schemes to create Extra Care provision, in partnership with health and social services, in order to meet the needs of a more frail client group. This programme has been accelerated recently with Department of Health funding available up to 2008 and is discussed further in 1.6 below and in Chapter 4. Other providers have either drifted towards allocating some difficult-to-let sheltered provision to other vulnerable groups, or have made a policy decision to take this route, considered further in Chapter 3.

Many providers have undertaken marketing and PR initiatives to publicise their smaller or harder to let sheltered flats, furnishing show flats and holding open days, supported by publicity material and advertisements which emphasise the benefits of small flats as being convenient and cheap to run. This can help in the short term by reducing voids, but does not solve providers' longer term dilemma about what to do with properties which, without significant investment, will not match the needs or aspirations of future customers. Providers should not overlook the fundamental importance of location: schemes which are difficult to access or are remote from amenities and transport links will not offer an attractive and independent lifestyle for an older person.

In addition to demanding a better quality environment, older people are now more likely to expect to be treated with respect and as a 'customer' by their landlord and by a professional scheme manager. Ageist, patronising and non-consultative approaches will increasingly be challenged and rejected by a more discerning client group. Future service users will have an increasingly diverse range of social, cultural, and health-related needs and expectations, and scheme managers must have the skills, knowledge and expertise to enable these to be met.

The Scottish Federation of Housing Associations 2005 Discussion Paper *Sheltered Housing's Future* looks at unsuitable buildings and unsuitable service configurations alongside a range of other challenges and uncertainties facing the sector, but reminds readers that sheltered housing remains a popular and successful option for many older people: *"If it was not acceptable, providers would not have long lists of people wanting to move to sheltered housing, and private developers would not still be building and selling it."*

❑ 1.3 Issues of tenure

In the 1970s and 1980s, sheltered housing providers had a ready pool of potential applicants who wished to move from their rented council house into rented sheltered housing. This has changed with the dramatic decline in the number of people living in rented accommodation, partly due to the impact of the right to buy from the 1980s onwards. Providers have been faced with rising void levels and choices to make regarding waiving or increasing capital limit thresholds. In 2001, 61 per cent of people aged 65 and over owned their homes outright as shown in the table below. The decline in the number of older renters is mirrored by an increased number of older owner occupiers who may look to private retirement housing for their future home.

Tenure of people living in households: by age, April 2001, Great Britain

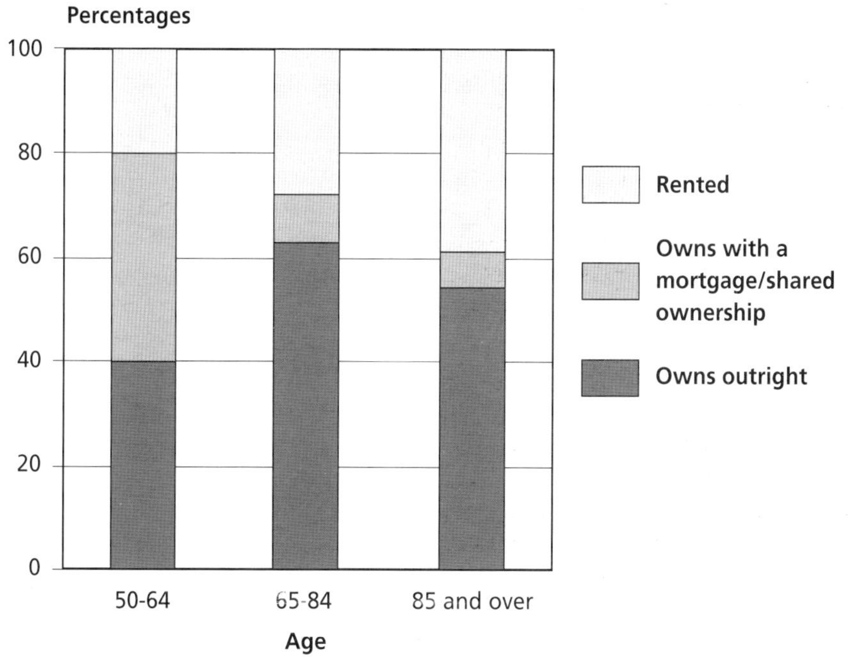

Reproduced from website of Age Concern England, www.ageconcern.org.uk

Mixed tenure sheltered and retirement housing schemes offer one way forward and reflect current thinking in the wider housing world regarding sustainable communities and regeneration. However, practical challenges remain to be resolved in developing and managing successful mixed tenure schemes for older people.

It will be important for policy-makers and housing providers to plan to meet the housing and support needs of this growing group of older owner-occupiers, for example in local strategies as discussed in 1.6 below.

Further issues for the retirement sector include the Commonhold and Leasehold Reform Act 2002 which could have considerable long-term implications. The act gives residents in leasehold properties (including retirement housing):

- The right to manage, ie take over the management of the property, without having to prove fault on the part of the landlord or pay their landlord compensation
- Improved consultation and resident rights, ie access to information regarding the management of their properties and giving more financial rights
- Collective enfranchisement, ie improved rights to purchase freeholds
- Commonhold – a new type of tenure that gives a share of the freehold.

At the time of writing, no retirement estates had exercised the right to manage but it is a strong incentive for managers to remain focused on their customers.

❑ 1.4 Key strategies influencing sheltered and retirement housing

With the older population increasing, planning for the current and future needs of older people has become a key part of government strategy. There has been a gradual but growing focus on older people, their views and needs, with an increased commitment to developing an overall strategy for older people. Wales is the first UK country to have developed and delivered an older people's strategy, and to have agreed to appoint a Commissioner for Older People.

The table opposite summarises recent government strategies relating to older people, and the key themes of relevance to sheltered and retirement housing providers.

Title of document, publishing government department, date	Overview of document	Key themes relevant to sheltered housing
Disability Discrimination Act 1995 (extended 2004)	Protects disabled people's rights in employment and education, in owning and managing property, and in accessing facilities, goods and services including housing	• Services must be offered (to prospective tenants) and provided in a non-discriminatory way – eg not treating disabled people differently • Schemes with communal facilities (eg lounges, scheme managers' offices, laundries) open to local community and/or outside groups must comply with Part 111: – remove restrictive features – provide signs accessible/ visible to people with sight impairments/wheelchair users
Home Alone – the role of housing in community care, Audit Commission, 1998	Identified local and national barriers to the effective delivery of housing aspects of community care	Heavily criticised sheltered housing's lack of: vision, strategy, service evaluation, effective joint working, statutory regulation regarding standards and performance Criticisms shaped subsequent reforms, see chapter 5, page 90 for more details
Quality and Choice for Older People's Housing: a strategic framework, DETR/ Department of Health, 2001	Two main objectives: 1. To ensure older people secure and sustain their independence 2. To support older people to make active and informed choices about their accommodation by providing access to appropriate housing and services and by providing advice on suitable services and options	Service approaches should be: integrated, inclusive, involving and preventative Five priority areas: • Diversity and choice • Information and advice • Flexible service provision • Quality • Joint working →

Title of document, publishing government department, date	Overview of document	Key themes relevant to sheltered housing
National Service Framework for Older People, Department of Health, 2001	A ten year programme linking services to promote independence and good health and set standards for older people's care across health and social services	Eight standards: 1. Age discrimination 2. Person centred care 3. Intermediate care 4. General hospital care 5. Stroke planning 6. Falls 7. Mental health 8. Health promotion
Housing for Older People, Housing Corporation, 2002	Sets out Corporation's broad approach for housing and services for older people in England	• Builds on the 5 priority areas in *Quality and Choice* • Remodelling to be an option in Approved Development Programme • Old Category 1 and 2 descriptions to disappear • Investment in sheltered housing that: – is based on the preferences of local people – will be appropriate to future demands – meets the objectives of the local strategy
Strategy for Housing Older People in England, Housing Corporation, 2003	Explains how Corporation will put the policy into practice	Lists 12 aims and associated measures and targets for older people's housing covering: 1. Anti-discriminatory approach 2. Age equality 3. Older people influencing decision-making 4. Older-people-friendly housing environments 5. Better housing advice 6. Effectiveness of adaptations 7. Development of culturally sensitive housing 8. Rural areas 9. Design 10. Clear descriptions in statistics 11. Increasing housing choices 12. Cutting delays in hospital discharge →

Title of document, publishing government department, date	**Overview of document**	**Key themes relevant to sheltered housing**
Definitions of housing association supported housing and housing for older people, Housing Corporation, 2004	To enable housing associations to categorise their housing for rent as either *general needs housing* or *supported housing* or *housing for older people* within the Housing Corporations' regulatory, data collection and investment systems	Removes the old Cat 1, Cat 2 terminology, replacing with: • Housing for older people (all special design features) • Housing for older people (some special design features) • Designated supported Housing for older people (no special design features)
Preparing Older People's Strategies, ODPM/ DH/ Housing Corporation, 2003	Guidance on developing local older people's strategies to ensure that housing is included in a consistent and unified manner	Framework for producing an older people's strategy; includes a sample template
Supporting People, ODPM and Administering Authorities, 1998 to present	Dozens of documents with guidance, instruction and strategy on older people. See in particular: • Administrative Guidance 2001 • Quality Assessment Framework 2004	Sheltered housing service should: • Meet local strategic objectives and demand • Demonstrate minimum quality standards and performance • Be cost effective • Continuously improve
Access and Capacity Systems Grant, Department of Health, 2004	Extra Care Housing Fund	Remodelling sheltered housing as Extra Care/very sheltered housing; new build Extra Care housing
Green Paper: Independence, Well-being and Choice – Our vision for the future of social care for adults in England, Department of Health, 2005	The vision includes: • Giving individuals greater choice and control over the way their needs are met • Enhancing the role of assistive technology and supported housing • A greater emphasis on prevention	• Greater emphasis on direct payments and individual budgets • Proposed introduction of the "right to request" not to live in a residential setting – could increase the demand for sheltered housing • Need to strengthen workforce skills and integration across sectors →

Title of document, publishing government department, date	Overview of document	Key themes relevant to sheltered housing
The Strategy for Older People in Wales, Welsh Assembly Government, 2003	Key areas: • Promoting positive ageing, tackling ageist discrimination • Work, learning and retirement • Health and wellbeing – integrated planning and service delivery • Appropriate support to promote and maintain independence	• Emphasis on high standard, joined up housing, health and social care services to maintain independence or make the transition to dependence • Unified health and social care assessment procedures • Initiatives to improve interplay of services around hospital admission or discharge
Housing for Older People, Social Justice and Regeneration Committee, National Assembly for Wales, 2004	Looks at current provision of housing for older people in Wales, and at what will be needed to cater for an ageing population	Specific recommendations for local housing strategies to cover: • The role of sheltered housing, including new leasehold, commonhold and shared ownership provision • Enhanced sheltered and Extra Care housing
Excluded Older People: Social Exclusion Unit Interim Report, ODPM, 2005	Identifies 3 main areas to address in tackling isolation and social exclusion among older people: • Early support and preventative services, rather than crisis interventions • Greater control and choice for older people • More joined up services	Sheltered housing will need to: • Ensure services meet new aspirations and needs • Demonstrate value by increasing opportunities for wider social inclusion and interaction – for residents and the wider community of older people • Demonstrate benefits to older people's mental and physical wellbeing
Opportunity Age: Meeting the challenge of ageing in the 21st century, DWP, 2005	Looks at the implications of changing demographics and the increased older population. Considers: • Age and employment • Active ageing in the community • Independence and security	Sheltered housing can address 3 key dimensions to independence – housing, neighbourhood and social activities With increasing emphasis on enabling older people to remain in their original homes, including proposed wider application of Lifetime Homes, sheltered housing will need actively to promote the additional benefits it offers

❑ 1.5 The implications of Supporting People for sheltered housing

The Supporting People programme provides the new operational and funding framework for delivering housing-related support services. It has resulted in some fundamental changes in the planning, management and day-to-day operation of rented sheltered housing, but has had less impact on private retirement housing, considered separately below. While Chapter 5 looks in detail at Supporting People, the key points are:

- **Strategy**
  Supporting People Commissioning Bodies across the country are responsible for devising local Supporting People strategies for service users, including older people. Local Supporting People strategies focus on health, housing, support and care for service users, within a context of empowerment, choice and control. Sheltered housing providers should now consider the role of their service in terms of implementing these strategies, and should ensure they are also taking account of other relevant strategies such as the local older people's strategy (see 1.6 below).
- **Quality Assessment Framework (QAF)**
  Services are assessed on the basis of how far they are able to meet the requirements of the Supporting People Quality Assessment Framework (QAF). The QAF identifies a range of core and supplementary objectives associated with good practice within sheltered housing. The framework is based on a process of self assessment and continuous review, and the ability of each service to meet a set of national standards will be one of the key elements in determining its future.
- **Contract**
  The support service in rented sheltered housing which was previously funded through housing benefit is now funded through Supporting People. All providers of rented sheltered housing must now contract with their local Supporting People Administering Authority (AA) in order to access Supporting People funding. Existing providers – local authorities and housing associations – received an interim contract at the commencement of the Supporting People regime in 2003 subject to the outcome of the first service reviews.
- **Review**
  Continuation of contracts will depend upon the review of all provision to be undertaken by each Administering Authority by March 2006.

■ Supporting People and leasehold retirement housing

Supporting People is administered in quite a different way within the retirement housing sector than it is within rented sheltered housing. Supporting People is purely a payments process to individual applicants who are deemed to qualify, and there are no contracts with providers, and no monitoring or review processes within retirement housing.

Individual leaseholders are required to claim Supporting People funding. Figures from the ODPM in 2004 show there are approximately 3,000 leaseholders claiming and receiving Supporting People payments, a figure which represents just under 3% of the total of those who live in leasehold retirement housing.

Prior to the introduction of the Supporting People programme, leaseholders were able to claim pension credit guarantee (formerly income support), and at the point of transition most claimants had immediate access to Supporting People for their support costs, with a guarantee that their current level of service would be maintained.

At the time of writing the government is reviewing payments procedures for leaseholders within the Supporting People programme. The view of the sector is that the increased bureaucracy is not justified, given the small number of claimants, and that, in any case, most estates were built without public grant.

■ The impact of Supporting People

The table opposite shows the impact of the Supporting People programme on all those who live in, work in, and manage rented sheltered housing.

The impact of Supporting People on all aspects of the service is explored throughout this Guide. Chapter 5 looks in detail at this new regime of regulation and accountability for sheltered housing. Chapter 2 explores the effects on the role of the scheme manager. Chapter 4 considers the increased need for partnership and collaborative working in terms of the changed environment and Chapter 6 looks at the key strategic role of the service manager in ensuring the future of the service.

The key themes of independence, empowerment and choice are of equal importance to all residents of housing for older people, regardless of tenure.

❑ 1.6 The support and care continuum for older people

It is increasingly clear that sheltered housing provision can no longer afford to exist in a vacuum. The process of re-thinking and re-modelling sheltered housing has to take place within the context of strategic planning and a clear analysis of local need. Older people's strategies now offer sheltered and retirement housing providers the opportunity to participate in a range of initiatives, designed to ensure local provision is tailored to local needs, and which aim to break down the barriers between housing, support and care.

Local older people's strategies and Supporting People Five Year strategies should define a continuum of provision designed to meet the current and projected needs

The impact of Supporting People on the sheltered housing service		
Supporting People requires the **Organisation/Service Manager** to deliver:	Supporting People requires the **Scheme Manager** to deliver:	Supporting People provides for **Scheme Residents** to have:
• A clear service strategy which – takes account of the Supporting People Five Year Strategy and local older people's strategy – demonstrates strategic relevance – encompasses diversity, fair access and inclusion • Robust policies, practices and procedures for the sheltered housing service, applied in all schemes and sensitive to the diverse needs of the local community • Support, training and information for all sheltered housing staff • Information, consultation and involvement for sheltered housing residents • A service which offers value for money, and which meets or exceeds minimum standards and performance indicators • A clear strategy for schemes with low demand/voids	• Excellent practice in service delivery • Informed implementation of policies, practices and procedures on a daily basis • Service designed to meet the needs of a diverse community and provide an appropriate, attractive and welcoming environment for all • Effective record keeping – providing an evidence trail • Encouragement and support of residents' involvement, independence, empowerment and choice • Regular one-to-ones with individual residents as part of the QAF assessment process, to determine and review support needs	• Clear information on all areas of service • Opportunity to feed back views on service delivery • Opportunities for involvement and participation at all levels • Regular interviews with scheme managers as part of the QAF needs and risk assessment process – with encouragement to express support needs

and demands of local older people. When planning for the future and preparing for their service reviews, providers should be aware of their local strategy, and should consider each scheme's place within it. However, not all authorities have yet developed strategies for older people, and this presents problems for providers wanting to plan ahead. The best strategies include a wide range of options and service users in their plans, highlighting the needs of the growing numbers living in the private sector, as well as the social rented sector.

Local strategies generally identify a number of ways in which housing and support services can support older people's independent living, including:

- In their original homes in the community, through the receipt of 'sheltered-type' support delivered through a community alarm service or floating support service such as a mobile warden service
- In sheltered or retirement housing, preferably which aims to offer a home for life
- Access to sheltered and Extra Care communal facilities for older people in the wider local community
- In Extra Care housing – in partnership with social services, care agencies and health services
- Through temporary placement in specially designated Intermediate Care schemes (or Intermediate Care flats in sheltered/Extra Care schemes) – in partnership with social and health services
- Home improvement agency services which provide support to older people in owner-occupied homes to enable them to improve and sustain their living environment and secure additional services to promote independent living.

There is considerable government support for the latter three initiatives in particular. While the Extra Care model has been in existence for some time, there is an increasing recognition that Extra Care sheltered and retirement housing can offer an alternative to residential care. Good sheltered and retirement housing provides a supported living environment for vulnerable adults that meets the independent living model, but avoids the need for residential care. This is increasingly being recognised by social care and health professionals and policy makers.

Reflecting this, the Department of Health set aside £29m in 2004/5 and £58m in 2005/6 to fund 1500 new places of Extra Care, and a further £60m for the period 2006-2008. One of the assessment and evaluation criteria for this Extra Care Housing Fund is evidence of strategic planning and needs analysis, underlining the importance of providers being aware of their local environment and how their own provision contributes to meeting current and future needs. Chapter 4 explores the partnership working and collaborative arrangements that are crucial to the success of such initiatives.

Extra Care sheltered housing

An Extra Care sheltered housing scheme provides housing for older people, in which either:

- in addition to scheme based support staff (traditionally called scheme manager or warden) a domiciliary care service is also available (normally based on site), *or*
- where a team providing care and support offers a sheltered housing style model of service delivery, including key 'support' tasks, traditionally defined as a 'warden type' service, alongside the personal care element.

Such schemes are normally purpose-built or have been rehabilitated for this purpose, aiming to provide a barrier free environment which facilitates mobility and access. Extra Care schemes may be rented or leasehold. Some Extra Care schemes offer special facilities for those suffering from mental frailty and dementia.

Names for this type of service provision vary, and may include Category 2½, Very Sheltered, Assisted Living or Frail Elders units.

Intermediate Care

Intermediate Care provides a short period (normally no longer than six weeks) of intensive rehabilitation and treatment to enable patients to return home following hospitalisation or to prevent admission to long term residential care; or intensive care at home to prevent unnecessary hospital admission. Provision can step up and step down, and should include a managed and supported return to home from designated flats or rooms in existing Extra Care or sheltered schemes.

The services people need to enable them to remain living independently are divided into three elements:

- **Housing** is provided by the landlord, funded by residents and/or housing benefit
- **Support** in sheltered housing is provided by the landlord, or subcontracted by the landlord to a specialist support provider, and is funded through Supporting People
- **Personal care** for those who qualify is funded and generally delivered through the social services and/or health budgets and delivered through a contracted service provider. Each social services department is required to publish their Fair Access to Care criteria (FACS) setting out which services they will provide and how these can be charged for.

In addition residents may receive a range of primary and secondary health care services.

Through the Supporting People programme, each older person living in rented sheltered housing should now go through a needs and risk assessment process, and have a support plan drawn up. Those receiving hands-on care should also have a care plan. The aim is to provide a seamless service in terms of delivery to the person receiving the services. Chapter 4 explores the importance of a partnership between all agencies involved to ensure that separate funding streams do not lead to a fragmented service. Of course, there still remains a need for nursing care for those older people who are simply too frail, mentally or physically, or too ill, to remain at home.

The diagram below shows the spectrum of services, the distinction between housing-related support and personal care, and also shows how Extra Care schemes and Intermediate Care provision frequently straddle the housing-care divide.

Housing-related support and personal and nursing care – the spectrum

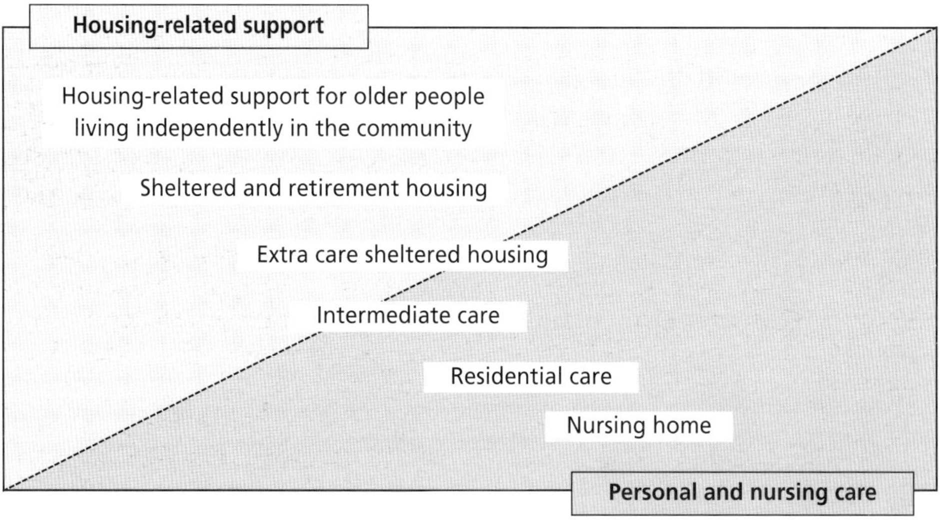

❑ 1.7 Overview

Demographic and cultural shifts, and changes in housing tenure, community care policies and related legislation have led to a more diverse, and, in many cases, older and frailer population living in, needing or wishing to live in sheltered and retirement housing. The service has therefore had to change. The old 'one-size-fits-all', service-led model has been replaced by a needs-led approach. Explicit values now underpin a modernised service, as illustrated by the following extract from a leaflet on sheltered housing:

StepForward

StepForward aims to enable older people to live independently through:

- Promoting independence and preventing the need for more intensive services
- Helping tenants to remain in their own homes for as long as they wish
- Empowering and involving tenants and promoting choice appropriate to cultural needs
- Creating a safe and secure home environment for tenants
- Assisting tenants to access and maintain support from external agencies when required
- Enabling tenants to establish supportive social networks
- Avoiding unnecessary/inappropriate hospital admission and promote early discharge
- Promoting integration with the surrounding community
- Responding appropriately in the event of an emergency
- Encouraging participation and involvement in the scheme
- Providing flexible services and facilities that meet the needs of all older people including those from black and ethnic minority groups.

StepForward is Metropolitan Housing Partnership's care and support service for vulnerable people.

This chapter has outlined the reasons why sheltered and retirement housing has changed and must continue to change, both in order to meet the aspirations and needs of an ageing and increasingly diverse population, and to meet today's emphasis on value for money, performance and user satisfaction. These issues are examined in more detail in the chapters which follow.

CHAPTER 2

THE EVER-CHANGING ROLE OF THE SCHEME MANAGER

Scheme managers are key players in the delivery of frontline services at a time of considerable change. This chapter focuses on their dynamic and continuously evolving role, and examines:

- The drivers for change
- The move from good neighbour to professional
- The resident/non-resident scheme manager debate
- Working beyond the sheltered scheme
- Advocacy and monitoring
- Promoting resident involvement and empowerment
- Sheltered housing schemes and the wider community
- Parameters and guidelines for the new and developing role
- Scheme managers and technology.

❑ 2.1 The drivers for change

The introduction of Supporting People in 2003 undoubtedly had a huge impact on the role of the scheme manager, and is fully explored in Chapter 5. Some providers had, however, already reviewed both the role and the service. These reviews were prompted by a range of factors, including:

- The increasingly competitive climate within housing
- The increase in local authority stock transfers – becoming an RSL required a re-think of all policies, practices and procedures
- The requirements of the Audit Commission and/or Housing Corporation inspection and regulation processes
- The process of accreditation with the CSHS Code of Practice for Sheltered Housing, which requires a thorough review of practices and procedures
- A realisation that the 'old' approaches to managing sheltered and retirement housing were no longer appropriate
- A commitment to provide services that meet the needs of existing residents and that will be attractive to potential service users.

❑ 2.2 From 'good neighbour' to well-trained professional

The traditional role of the scheme manager has changed, and continues to do so, as sheltered and retirement housing meets an increasing range of client needs. The original resident warden role has gradually shifted to that of a scheme manager, who may live on- or off-site. The old 'good neighbour' role has been replaced by an emphasis on delivering a good quality, professional service, and supporting independence, choice and control for older people.

Saxon Weald Housing Association

Following stock transfer, Saxon Weald thoroughly modernised the role of its sheltered housing staff. The key differences between the past and present role are:

	Then:	Now:
Residential status:	• Lived in a flat on the scheme, with a service or tied tenancy	• Live off site, with an assured tenancy
Hours:	• 21 hour day	• 37 hour week
Role:	• Friendly neighbour	• Professional worker
Technology:	• Warden Call system	• Up-to-date technology and out-of-hours control centre
Training:	• Basic training	• Training needs recognised and regularly reviewed
Work situation:	• Isolated	• Team members
Social activities with residents:	• Called the bingo	• Encourage and promote resident involvement and participation

Scheme managers are now recognised as professionals, and benefit from further positive changes:

- Delegated scheme budgets for which they have control
- On-scheme computers – access to the internet, and the organisation's intranet where policies and practices can be easily downloaded
- Carrying out assessments of applicants and involvement in allocation
- Monthly one-to-ones with their line manager
- Personal development reviews
- Coaching and encouragement
- Rewards offered to staff for new ideas.

Debates at conferences and elsewhere show that, while many employers have implemented similar changes, others have not yet begun. A further issue stressed by scheme managers is that, as well as adapting to their own changed role, it is a challenge to ensure the changes are recognised and understood by colleagues, other agencies, residents and their families. This challenge was the driver for the creation of the Emerging Role of the Warden project 1996, which then became ERoSH from 1998.

It is increasingly important that scheme managers are trained and knowledgeable, able to work effectively with residents, their relatives and carers, and in collaborative partnership with a range of statutory and voluntary organisations. They must be flexible and adaptable in their approach, in order to keep up with the rapid pace of change. This can only be achieved through:

- Acceptance of the importance and relevance of the role
- Recognition by other professionals, particularly in the wider housing, health and social care sectors
- The support of line managers
- A commitment to professionalism by the employing organisation reflected within areas such as training and service development.

❑ 2.3 Resident or non-resident manager?

In the early days of sheltered housing, the residential status of the scheme manager was universal and unquestioned. Over recent years increasing numbers of providers have recognised the pressures of living on-site and other disadvantages of tied accommodation for scheme managers. In recruitment terms, a requirement for resident staff can limit the pool of candidates who have the right abilities and are prepared to give up their homes in order to live 'over the shop'. Some providers have therefore moved towards a non-residential, frequently nine-to-five, scheme manager service. Out-of-hours cover for residents is provided using the available – increasingly sophisticated – technology, via social alarm control centres and/or a visiting, peripatetic or mobile warden service.

For such changes to take place smoothly and with the minimum of negative impact on service users, a great deal of consultation and preparation is required. There are particular problems for leasehold providers in terms of moving towards a non-resident manager, since the lease that residents signed is likely to state that they are paying for the services of a 'resident manager'. Even if, following resident consultation, such a change is agreed, it is likely to require a variation to the lease requiring the agreement of 100% of residents.

SLFHA

Following problems recruiting to residential scheme manager posts SLFHA organised consultation on moving to a non-resident scheme manager service. All tenants were invited to meetings in the communal lounges of their schemes, where the recruitment difficulties were explained:

- The stress of 'living on the job'
- Applicants' reluctance to give up secure accommodation
- The impact of the European Working Time Directive which meant that a scheme manager, even if living on-site, could no longer be expected to work during the day and also be on call in the evenings and at weekends.

Once tenants better understood the need for change, they agreed that the posts could be advertised as non-resident. This agreement was assisted by the fact that residents had been impressed by the reliable service provided by the agency staff covering some SLFHA schemes at that time on a non-residential basis.

Out-of-hours cover for SLFHA schemes is now provided by a social alarm control centre.

McCarthy & Stone plc

An independent study was commissioned in 2003 to explore the attitudes of prospective and current residents and their families towards the role of the resident House Manager in McCarthy & Stone category II private sheltered housing developments.

Headline findings of the research can be summarised as follows:

- Residents value the resident House Manager more highly than do prospective residents – typically due to having a working knowledge of the role once they have moved in.
- Almost two-thirds of prospective and existing residents felt that resident House Managers were always needed in McCarthy & Stone retirement housing.
- Existing residents who felt that a resident House Manager was not always needed typically lived in developments with a day manager.
- Families rated the House Manager more highly than did either existing or prospective residents.
- Families had much higher expectations of the role of the House Manager than had either prospective or existing customers.

→

- Families were inclined to expect the House Manager to provide assistance in an emergency (92%) and ensure the general upkeep of scheme (88%).
- Families were almost universal in feeling that the cost of the House Manager did not outweigh the benefits – a figure just below that reported by residents.
- The majority of families felt that a resident House Manager was always needed in retirement housing.
- Consistent with the above finding, families were least likely to favour McCarthy & Stone building developments without a resident House Manager.

The research indicates that there will always remain a proportion of people who will only accept a resident House Manager in retirement developments. These will typically be those aged over 75, although not exclusively so.

Bristol City Council

When a scheme manager post becomes vacant, an evaluation of the scheme is carried out in order to determine its future, including whether it is suitable for a non-resident manager post. The evaluation includes:

- An analysis of the care and support needs of existing residents
- The scheme design, location and layout
- The costs involved in bringing the scheme up to standard for residents with medium to high support needs.

Depending upon the results of the evaluation, consultation takes place with residents about proposed changes. Bristol has found that such change is more likely to be accepted by residents if the consultation is open and honest, and, where a non-resident manager is being proposed, reassurances are given about the provision of an efficient and timely out-of-hours response.

There are still providers which require their scheme managers to continue to live on-site, and to provide cover for out-of-hours emergencies, and this is frequently the stated preference of residents. However, what has changed is the implicit assumption that, by providing accommodation, the employer can expect the scheme manager to be on call at night and during the weekends to deal with issues occurring on the scheme, after having worked a 'normal' day. Where this meant resident staff were working excessive hours, challenges by groups of scheme managers have resulted in such practices being ruled as unacceptable. The 'Harrow Judgment' is a particularly well-known example.

The Working Time Regulations and the Harrow Judgment

Employers must be clear about the implications of the Working Time Regulations for residential scheme staff, and should be aware of the way these were interpreted within what is now known as the 'Harrow Judgment':

The Working Time Regulations

The key employee rights:

- Average 48 hour week
- Rest break – 20 minutes in any 6 hours
- Weekly rest – 24 hours in any week/48 hours in a fortnight
- Annual leave

The on-call position:
Employees are working if they are:

- At their employer's disposal
- Carrying out work activity or duties
- Receiving relevant training

The 'Harrow Judgment'

Davies et al v LB Harrow was an employment tribunal decision made in 2003, which stated that resident scheme managers working for Harrow had been 'at work' beyond their contracted 37 hours per week because they were not allowed to leave the scheme when they were on call.

Harrow was found to be contravening the Working Time Regulations, since:

- The workplace was found to include the tied accommodation occupied by staff
- The employees were working both while dealing with out-of-hours emergencies *and* while on-call (since they were required to be in the flat and near the phone), and
- The on-call hours meant that the staff did not have the required 11 hour rest periods between shifts.

As they were deemed to have been working for up to 76 hours per week on top of their contracted 37 hours they had also been paid below the minimum wage.

The Harrow staff were paid compensation for this breach of the regulations, and of course their terms and conditions were revised in the light of this judgment.

While the situation at Harrow may be different from that of other providers, nevertheless, this judgment and those made in other, similar cases serve as a warning to providers which require staff to remain on call. Employers should seek legal advice where there is any doubt at all, to ensure they are not contravening the Working Time Regulations. Similarly, staff who feel their conditions of employment may be breaching these regulations should consult their trade union.

Along with other factors, a greater awareness of the Working Time Regulations has prompted many providers to re-examine their scheme managers' role and accommodation status. It is important, however, that this issue is considered more widely than in employment terms alone. Removing the resident scheme manager can impact upon the service promise to residents, particularly that of a 'home for life'. The service which replaces the resident scheme manager during the night and over the weekends needs to be of the same quality. While the control centre will deal with the emergency call, the on-site response, where it is needed, should ideally be provided by a trained mobile warden or floating support worker.

Removing the resident post has particular implications for the increasing numbers of frail residents or those suffering from dementia, who frequently require support out-of-hours. The needs and risk assessment and support planning process is important in identifying those needs which go beyond what Supporting People can fund, and which require collaborative working with health and/or social services.

Clearly there are cost implications in relation to on-scheme changes such as this, and residents must have the opportunity to be consulted as to the range of options.

❑ 2.4 Working beyond the sheltered scheme

In addition to the increasing number of off-site scheme managers, there is a move towards a wider approach to the role of the scheme manager. Whether or not they have residential status, it is no longer necessarily the case that scheme managers work only with the service users living at one particular scheme. Increasing numbers are working outside the boundaries of the scheme with older clients throughout the community, whether in provision managed by their own organisation, or in owner-occupied or rented private sector accommodation in the local area. This offers some of the advantages of living in sheltered housing to a wider range of clients, giving them support as well as access to social activities in the sheltered scheme itself. It also provides an additional income stream for providers.

Some of these initiatives have been set up in response to emerging local older people's strategies, in which Supporting People Commissioning Bodies have identified a need for support to isolated older people living in the wider community. While meeting this need, the organisation concerned is able to demonstrate added value in terms of its sheltered housing provision – a key factor in securing the future of the service. Other initiatives have come from Best Value reviews.

Selby District Council, as part of its review of the warden service, piloted an outreach team working from a base in the community, incorporating support plans, ensuring that service users receive an efficient and effective service. The service has now been extended, with support officers working from bases throughout the district in teams of four or five.

Woking Borough Council reorganised its sheltered housing staff into three peripatetic teams in anticipation of Supporting People. A pilot 'enhanced' service to a group of tenants offers social and emotional support such as assisting older people to get out and about within the neighbourhood and encouraging cooking skills for people who lack them.

Hillingdon Homes provides a visiting service to council tenants aged over 60 living near its sheltered schemes. Sheltered housing managers act as housing advocates, assisting clients with repairs reporting, benefit forms, and referrals to other agencies. In addition, tenants are encouraged to join in the social events and outings organised at the sheltered housing.

Slough Borough Council revised the support services delivered to older people living in sheltered housing and in the wider community following a Best Value review. Slough found that its wider community services were insufficient to meet the needs of many service users. Conversely, not every sheltered housing scheme resident needed the more comprehensive service offered to them. The service revisions aimed to correct this imbalance.

Following resident consultation, Slough introduced a new Supported Housing Service. Former wardens now work in teams of Supported Housing Officers, along with other welfare and care staff. Teams are responsible for serving all the tenants in their area within the Borough, encompassing tenants in sheltered schemes and tenants in the wider community. Supported Housing Officers are thus benefiting a much larger community than before, and delivering an equitable, high-quality, needs-led service to all the tenants on their patch.

❑ 2.5 Advocacy and monitoring

Increasing numbers of residents – as many as 60% in some sheltered schemes – now receive domiciliary care to enable them to remain independent. This means that advocacy on behalf of residents, together with monitoring of, and liaison with, the domiciliary care provider are now a crucial aspect of the scheme manager's wider role. ERoSH has produced a good practice leaflet which recommends that sheltered and retirement housing staff develop a thorough working knowledge of the key regulations and standards governing domiciliary care. This will *"enable sheltered and retirement housing staff to raise concerns, drive quality improvements and identify gaps and weaknesses"*.

However, the ambiguity of this aspect of the scheme manager's role has been highlighted in a recent report examining the role of care teams in sheltered housing:

> *"The scheme manager might act as an advocate for a resident, on request taking up cases of poor service provision, facilitating access to statutory bodies or to voluntary organisations etc. Or they might play a more proactive role, urging the resident to seek support, perhaps through facilities hitherto unknown to the resident.*
>
> *Monitoring might take the form of casually noting the arrival and departure of care workers; alternatively it could involve recording the exact times of arrival and departure or the regular checking of the log book held by the resident."*
>
> (from *A Care Team for Sheltered/Retirement Housing – Report*, University of Sussex, September 2004)

In addition, within Extra Care schemes in particular, there may be times when the scheme manager takes on delegated authority from one of the key partners to make emergency assessments, to alter a care plan or to direct care workers on-site.

For this growing area of work for scheme managers it is therefore essential that:

- The responsibilities of scheme managers with regard to advocacy and monitoring are clarified, both within job descriptions and with key partners
- Scheme managers are equipped with the skills, understanding and knowledge to undertake:
  - the specific tasks of advocacy and monitoring
  - the wider aspects of joint and collaborative working
- Training and support offered to scheme managers reflects this aspect of the developing role.

As Chapter 4 demonstrates, collaborative working arrangements are increasingly necessary to ensure that older people receive a service which meets their needs. Chapter 3 stresses the importance of partnerships when working with diverse groups of service users. Both the scheme manager and their line manager must work hard to achieve these links, with the scheme manager frequently maintaining liaison at operational level with colleagues in other agencies, while the higher level managers develop strategic partnerships.

❑ 2.6 Promoting resident involvement and empowerment

Scheme managers have a crucial role to play in promoting resident involvement, choice and control. The concept of resident involvement in sheltered housing has moved on considerably in recent years. Once, sheltered housing residents were deemed to be 'participating' if they attended a coffee morning, and 'success' in terms of participation was judged by how many people attended such social events. Now, regulatory bodies share high expectations of organisations in terms of participation and involvement outcomes, and sheltered housing is included within this expectation. It has become essential for organisations to ensure that older residents are given every opportunity for involvement in a range of activities and at a range of levels. The key objective within this process, for both individuals and the community is that of empowerment (individual and collective) ultimately leading to choice and control for residents.

The table below illustrates the stages in this process, the input needed from scheme managers and the benefits for residents on an individual or group basis.

'Ladder of empowerment through involvement' (inspired by Arnstein's 'Ladder of Participation', 1969) – ***readers should start at the bottom (level 0) and read upwards***

Level of involve-ment	Key activities and role of scheme manager	Skills/approach required by scheme manager	Outcomes for residents/scheme
6	Residents, either in small focus groups, or as individuals are encouraged and supported to comment on the organisation's policies, practices and service delivery; opportunities for participation in formal consultation structures are made clear, and support is given to enable this to happen.	All skills previously identified, plus a good understanding of opportunities and structures for participation that exist within the organisation, including complaints procedures.	Residents feel valued – their opinions count; they are empowered to participate at all levels in terms of formal and informal structures, plus they can if they wish participate in a range of social and recreational opportunities based on their choices.
5	Alongside group discussions as in (3), below, scheme manager also enables each resident (through the needs and risk assessment/ support planning process) to identify and express their individual needs and aspirations on a one-to-one basis.	As noted in 4 below, plus empathy; ability to 'hear' individually expressed needs and aspirations, and relate these to local resources.	**All** residents are encouraged and enabled to identify needs and choices, and to express their views, including those who do not participate currently/find it hard to contribute in a group etc. →

Level of involve-ment	Key activities and role of scheme manager	Skills/approach required by scheme manager	Outcomes for residents/scheme
4	Scheme manager creates a range of opportunities for residents – either as one large group, or in smaller groups – to say what they would like by way of social and recreational activities, both on and off scheme; involvement of residents in organising activities is encouraged; 'regulars' continue to play a role, but others are also brought on board.	Listening, questioning, resource investigation and meeting-chairing skills; knowledge of local options, opportunities and resources, plus enhanced levels of organisational, communication and delegation skills as noted in 3, 2 and 1 below.	Potential involvement of a wider range of residents; ideas encouraged; improved self-esteem and confidence; greater likelihood of developing participation by some residents in wider issues relating to the management of the organisation, feedback on service provision etc.
3	Scheme manager consults with residents (frequently a small group of 'regulars', 'the committee' or those who are most forthcoming or vociferous) about a limited range of options for social activities.	As below, plus communication skills.	Residents who are involved benefit from being able to express their views; however those who are not part of the 'inner circle' may feel excluded.
2	Residents help scheme manager run social activities (eg by setting tables, washing up, choosing destinations for trips etc).	As below, plus limited delegation skills.	Residents who are involved benefit from feeling useful/ needed.
1	Some limited activities take place, chosen and directed by scheme manager (eg, bingo, coffee morning, coach trip).	Some organisa-tional skills.	Residents who attend benefit from some social contact.
0	No activities involving residents take place.	0	0

Scheme and service managers should not assume that a scheme can make a single jump from level 2 or even level 3 on the ladder – which is where many managers feel that they are at present – to level 6, the top rung. A gradual approach is not only required, but is more likely to ensure lasting change. Consultation and involvement with regard to policies, practices and service delivery is unlikely to be successful unless level 4 has been reached and consolidated – and many scheme managers feel that their biggest challenge is the move from level 3 to 4. Progressing up this ladder by working with older people both individually and in groups and ensuring their views and opinions are valued, helps to develop older residents' confidence and willingness to be further involved. As a result, some are more likely to become involved in participation structures at an organisational level, explored in Chapter 6.

The needs and risk assessment and support planning processes provide an excellent opportunity for developing each individual's potential to get involved. To facilitate this, scheme managers must be well trained in enabling residents to articulate their wider needs and aspirations. Scheme managers can then relate these to local resources and increased opportunities for participation in the life of the scheme and local community.

One useful tool, available free of charge from ERoSH, provides a series of carefully designed questions which can enable a diverse range of service users to express their needs and aspirations. The extract below focuses on social involvement, and four further topics are covered in the Plan.

Extract from ERoSH Sheltered Housing Model Support Plan 2004

Social involvement

- Do you join in scheme events? (Are you aware when they take place and how they are notified?)
- Do you belong to any outside clubs or organisations?
- Do you get on well with your neighbours?
- Can you think of any ways that socialising could be made easier for you?
- Are there any activities that you would like to see run in this scheme?
- Are there any activities that you would like to be involved in organising for this scheme?

The scheme manager needs support, encouragement and training in order to build real involvement at scheme level. Chapter 6 looks at the key role of the service manager in:

- Supporting scheme managers to develop resident involvement at their schemes

- Ensuring that appropriate skills are developed to enhance resident involvement and empowerment, providing training where required
- Ensuring opportunities are available for residents to participate at higher levels, building on the existing levels of involvement developed by scheme managers.

❑ 2.7 Sheltered housing schemes and the wider community

Many scheme managers carry out wider community development work in addition to promoting scheme residents' involvement. Beyond the scheme, the scheme manager has an important role to play in promoting active ageing, encouraging older people's awareness of and participation in issues and activities taking place in the wider community. Making links with local groups, putting ideas to residents and matching individuals' skills with relevant activities are all part of this process.

Promoting awareness of issues outside the scheme can also help move towards opening up the sheltered scheme to the wider community. Implementing this successfully calls for partnership working, explored further in Chapter 4, between sheltered housing providers, tenants, their families and local non-statutory agencies and communities.

There is no formal obligation to develop interaction with the wider community, but where it is already taking place, residents of both rented and leasehold schemes benefit greatly from a number of positive factors associated with greater integration between their schemes and the local area, for example:

- Older people from the local community, their relatives and carers are encouraged to become familiar with the scheme, which in the longer term may increase demand.
- Communal areas can offer a much-needed meeting place, especially in rural locations.
- Opportunities for interaction between older residents and local schoolchildren are created, to the mutual benefit of all.
- Partnership arrangements, such as those between the provider and voluntary organisations, local authority social services departments etc, can also benefit residents, eg leisure activities on schemes, use of the scheme as a base for home care staff, day care, lunch clubs etc.
- Residents themselves may be keen to increase attendance at social events, or simply to widen their horizons.

Discussion and consultation are crucial if residents are to feel comfortable with the process of opening up their communal areas to the wider community. Privacy and security issues must be considered. An awareness of the needs of the community outside the scheme, coupled with a recognition that they, as individuals, have much to offer, can influence residents' willingness to open up schemes for a range of shared activities, as shown in the case study below.

Charter Housing

Charter Housing is one of seven housing providers which participated in the CSHS 'Lifelong Learning and Active Ageing Project'. This two-year European-funded project supported sheltered housing schemes to develop ways of enabling and encouraging older people to use their time, patience and life skills in the communities around their schemes. Although Charter already had a good record of involving its older residents, the sheltered schemes which participated in the project had no previous history of opening their doors to the wider community.

Charter's Learning Links project worker tried a number of ways of integrating the residents of Pant-y-Celyn sheltered scheme with the outside community. She began by making contact with a wide range of local groups and agencies with whom the residents might wish to link, at the same time finding out what skills and knowledge and ideas the residents had that they might wish to contribute.

Ideas for various activities were put to the scheme residents for discussion, but the one that caught everyone's interest was for a class of school students (15 and 16 year-olds) with learning support needs to visit the scheme to help the residents with some fundraising activities for the local hospice. Although the residents were slightly intimidated when the young lads first arrived at the scheme, the relationship soon became one of mutual support. The young people helped the older people with computer skills. Some of the older men used their previous workplace experience to give mock job interviews to help the students understand what to expect when they left school – invaluable preparation in an area of high unemployment.

Positive outcomes from the young people's regular visits to the scheme encouraged some residents to express an interest in becoming involved with the wider community in further ways, including:

- Through links made with local ethnic minority women's groups, it was discovered that there was a need for female 'chaperones' for women whose culture would not allow them to have driving lessons from a male instructor, as this would mean being alone with a man to whom they were not related. One resident was happy to take on this task, and also began helping the women with the driving theory test.
- Links with asylum seekers' groups resulted in another resident, a former keen cyclist, using his skills to help a group of asylum seekers to build and repair bicycles, using cast-off spares and abandoned bikes, enabling each of the asylum seekers to benefit from building their own bike at no cost.

→

- Links with social services and voluntary groups offering support to young people leaving care showed that many youngsters struggled to manage by themselves, since they did not know how to cook or to budget. This led to some of the scheme residents becoming involved in 'Cheap as Chips' days, in which residents and young people joined together to cook and eat cheap and nutritious meals, with older people passing on cooking skills, recipes and budgeting hints.

Pant-y-Celyn residents have greatly benefited from the increased confidence and sense of self worth which has resulted from their involvement with these activities.

At the 2004 UK Housing Awards the Learning Links Project won the 'Outstanding Achievement in Social Housing, Wales' award and was also the overall UK winner of the 'Outstanding Achievement in Social Housing'.

Where a landlord decides to encourage wider use of its schemes, this must be managed in a robust and transparent manner, as demonstrated in the following example.

Pennine Housing 2000

Pennine had been committed for some time to the principle of encouraging wider use of its sheltered housing schemes. However, previous arrangements were ad hoc, and at times caused tensions between tenants and 'outsiders'. Following wider consultation on a range of service-related issues, Pennine worked with residents to develop a policy on the use of communal lounges. The policy was based on the wider benefits to both sheltered residents and local communities of opening up schemes, as recommended in good practice guidelines, as well as on existing residents' views.

Key points of the policy included:

- *That facilities are available to older people in the community (informally or to groups or organisations like Age Concern) as well as sheltered tenants*
- *That Social Services can continue to have their Home Care offices in the schemes as this helps joint working*
- *That Pennine can also make use of facilities eg for staff meetings, for other local Tenants Associations to meet etc*
- *That new users are not given priority over sheltered tenants*
- *That the Sheltered Officer teams manage the facilities and usage*
- *That detailed guidelines are drawn up, in consultation with tenants, including some rules for charging non-sheltered users*

and sheltered residents took part in a focus group to devise guidelines for implementing the policy.

❑ 2.8 Parameters and guidelines for the new and developing role

■ Job descriptions

Changing roles require job descriptions to be revised and rewritten so that the purpose of the role within the new climate is clear. As well as encompassing the new tasks and the professionalism required, the skills and knowledge needed to do the job must be clearly spelt out in the person specification. The sample extracts below are from job descriptions revised by a range of sheltered housing providers.

Scheme managers' job descriptions: Key extracts

- Provide professional quality support services to enable older people to live independently, either in their original homes or in a sheltered housing scheme.
- Liaise with statutory and voluntary agencies to ensure appropriate co-ordinated care and support is delivered to the Association's tenants to enable independent living.
- Promote and enable social and leisure activities within the scheme for both residents and other older people living in the local neighbourhood.
- Effectively manage sheltered housing schemes and services to ensure that older people are provided with a safe, supportive and balanced environment.
- Participate in the development of the sheltered housing service, and strengthen its role within the wider community care context.
- Facilitate the provision of extra support and personal care through liaison with voluntary and statutory agencies.
- Contribute to meeting the Association's and Commissioning Authority's performance targets.
- Ensure the implementation of good practice and continuous improvement within sheltered housing, responding positively to challenges to meet the requirement of the Supporting People Reviews.

SLFHA

SLFHA, part of Horizon Housing Group, has identified the following key competencies required to carry out the revised role, and tests for these when appointing new scheme managers:

- Communication
- Leadership
- Ethical behaviour
- Problem-solving
- Business awareness
- Teamwork
- Customer focus

SLFHA also expects scheme managers to have or to commit to undertake the following: National Housing Certificate, ECDL (European Computer Driving Licence) and Red Cross First Aid four-day course (equivalent qualifications are accepted).

While the generic skills required by rented and leasehold sheltered scheme managers are almost identical, some of the knowledge requirements relating to the two roles are increasingly divergent. For example, retirement housing managers need:

- A good knowledge of issues relating to the leases which are in place at the scheme where they work
- An understanding of the process of buying and selling the properties within their scheme
- An understanding of the rights of leaseholders
- An understanding of how Supporting People applies to leaseholders.

Scheme managers in rented housing need:

- An understanding of how the Supporting People programme operates locally
- A good knowledge of the Supporting People QAF
- The ability to achieve the QAF minimum standards at their scheme.

■ Ensuring the changed role is fully understood

It is important that scheme managers are well supported by their line managers in ensuring that their role is well understood by residents, residents' relatives and all outside agencies. A team approach works best here, where members of staff at all levels take every opportunity to ensure that others understand how sheltered housing, and the role of those who work within it, has changed. This is explored further in Chapter 6.

The example below demonstrates how the scheme manager's work can assist colleagues and partner agencies as well as sheltered residents.

Home Housing Group

Two scheme managers at Home Housing North West gave presentations to colleagues and tenants in order to raise awareness and broaden understanding of their role, set out in the points below.

- *We work with the most frail, vulnerable, and sometimes demanding tenants the organisation has.*
- *We participate in management decision-making in collaboration with colleagues and our Management Team, and in consultation with our tenants; we are actively involved in forming our strategies.*
- *By making referrals on behalf of our tenants to external agencies and working in partnership, we are able to co-ordinate support services into the schemes appropriate to our tenants' needs.*

- *We monitor the rent accounts, and try to minimise void periods.*
- *Through networking within our own organisation and with other service providers, we try to make sure that our tenants' needs are met in the most appropriate way. In doing so, we have been able to involve the wider community, and promote the sheltered units and the organisation. Other older people and external agencies now use many of our communal facilities, to provide services both to the schemes and externally.*
- *Creating an interest in the community towards our schemes has had a positive effect on allocations and re-letting. We find that a substantial amount of applications arrive by word of mouth. We accompany prospective tenants viewing properties and process the applications.*
- *We provide confidential advice and information on a range of benefits, and with the inception of Supporting People some of us also provide assistance to older people living outside the sheltered units, in category 1 properties.*
- *We are involved with marketing initiatives, some led from the schemes and others at different venues. This has proved very successful in promoting the organisation.*
- *We are aware of health and safety issues, in and around our schemes and again we work closely with other internal departments to make sure our equipment and common areas meet an acceptable standard and comply with current legislation.*
- *We maintain daily contact with our tenants, either in person or by using an intercom system, to monitor their wellbeing, and give support when needed.*
- *By receiving and reporting repairs, we are able to advise tenants on the response times, and monitor the progress of contractors.*
- *Ongoing training is paramount to our continued development and we are actively involved in varied training programmes.*

■ Manuals and codes of conduct

Along with changing and more complex roles comes the need to clarify boundaries, and to offer clear guidance to staff. This is particularly important for scheme managers as members of a dispersed workforce who are working with vulnerable clients. Supporting People lays down clear standards for service delivery; it is the scheme manager who implements these on a day-to-day basis, and this cannot be done without a framework of clear guidance relating to organisational policies and practice.

Scheme managers' manuals

Manuals or handbooks are a key tool that helps scheme managers do their job. As well as containing all the policies, procedures and service standards that are relevant to the sheltered housing service, they also usually contain the forms, vital contact details and other reference materials used by scheme managers on a day-to-day basis. Such manuals need to be devised, presented and maintained in a way which ensures ownership of them by scheme managers. They must be a handy, frequently used reference tool for scheme managers, and not (as sometimes happens) a large volume containing out-of-date policies which sits gathering dust on a shelf. Where all scheme managers are online it is easier to ensure everyone is working to the current policy.

Developing manuals

SLFHA's scheme managers' manual covers all the areas of the scheme manager's role. All scheme managers can access the manual online, and are encouraged not to print out a copy because the material is periodically updated and it is important that they are working from the current version. There is a programme of review in which scheme managers participate, mainly working in groups or pairs within team meetings.

The London Borough of Sutton needed to revise its existing procedure guide as part of the requirements for accreditation with the CSHS Code of Practice for Sheltered Housing. To ensure their ownership of the guide, scheme managers were fully involved in the process, from brainstorming the areas that the guide should cover, to working up the chapters with support from colleagues in other council departments.

Loreburn HA ensured that its residents had the opportunity to comment during the development of the warden's manual. The manual was developed by a working group consisting of the housing manager, housing officer and wardens from each complex. The draft document was made available for comment to all sheltered tenants, either in hard copy or through online access using the computers provided by Loreburn at each scheme.

Good practice checklist: Producing relevant and useful manuals

Manuals must be:

- ✓ Relevant to the scheme manager's daily work;
- ✓ Easy to access, either in paper format or online
- ✓ Underpinned by the service training programme
- ✓ 'Owned' by those who use them
- ✓ Updated and reviewed with the full involvement of their users along with other stakeholders

Codes of conduct for scheme managers

Today's high expectations of scheme managers, and the increasing emphasis on professionalism, requires a set of clear parameters regarding behaviour and attitudes in the workplace. Given the vulnerable nature of the client group in sheltered housing, a code of conduct offers valuable protection to clients and employees alike.

Derby Homes

Derby Homes' staff handbook has a section on the scheme manager role, which includes specific guidance setting out clear personal/professional boundaries for all scheme managers. This guidance complements Derby Homes' corporate employee code of conduct. The issues covered are:

- Personal integrity
- Personal relationships with tenants and with colleagues
- Professional appearance
- Substance misuse
- Personal profit or gain
- Limits to confidentiality
- Reporting suspected abuse.

❑ 2.9 Scheme managers and technology

As with many other aspects of the scheme manager's role, there are wide differences in access to personal computers on schemes. The fact that scheme managers are members of a dispersed workforce makes access to IT even more important – they can benefit from the instant communication method which emailing offers, they can download organisational documents from an intranet, and they can produce professional correspondence, notes and case studies about work-based issues.

In other words, scheme managers whose employers provide access to personal computers are recognised as full members of the organisation's professional workforce. To quote one scheme manager:

> *"The email system has greatly improved the communication for scheme managers. It can sometimes seem like a very isolated job, and to be in touch with the rest of your work colleagues is very important. Even a shared joke can brighten your day."*

Good practice checklist: Key features of IT provision for scheme managers

- ✓ All scheme managers have their own laptop or computer and printer.
- ✓ Support is provided by in-house IT staff to ensure competence in internet use, emailing and word processing.
- ✓ A dedicated telephone line and/or the use of broadband ensures access to internet/intranet services at all times.
- ✓ Scheme managers produce professional notices, posters and correspondence.
- ✓ Scheme managers report all non-urgent repairs to the repairs team via email, as well as ordering cleaning consumables and stationery requirements.
- ✓ Scheme managers have access to the rents database, so they can check rents regularly and pick up on potential problems at an early stage.
- ✓ Scheme managers keep a spreadsheet of all clients on which they record information such as when each visit is completed, and what services clients receive – these contribute to monthly statistical returns.
- ✓ Scheme managers have access to the same documents and information as office-based staff *at the same time*.
- ✓ All standard policies, procedures and forms relating to sheltered housing and the scheme manager's role are available via intranet sites.
- ✓ Central control information is relayed via email, substantially cutting down on the paperwork required.
- ✓ Access to the internet enables items to be bought for schemes via mail order and enables scheme managers to search the internet for information on support services and agencies.

However, there are still many organisations which do not yet recognise the importance of ensuring equality between scheme staff who deliver services at the front line, and office-based staff, for the majority of whom the prospect of carrying out their job without access to a personal computer would be unthinkable.

■ Assistive technology and telecare

While scheme managers as an occupational group may lag behind in terms of access to personal computers, they have been using increasingly sophisticated technology in the form of social alarm systems for many years. These have evolved from the simple scheme-based warden call systems of the 1970s, through the increasing use of central control technology in the 1980s to today's 'intelligent' second and third generation systems. These devices have the potential to monitor activity and environment, as well as to act as a means of communication.

The use of assistive technology within sheltered housing is now virtually universal. It is taken for granted as one of the key factors both within and outside sheltered and retirement housing which supports older people with independent living. Its use in terms of the health care agenda is increasing through partnership initiatives. The Department of Health has set aside a £80m grant fund for telecare and electronic assistive technology for the period 2006-2008. This money will be available to social services authorities working with their local strategic partners, including housing and community alarm providers.

The benefits of assistive technology for service users with dementia and other mental health problems are explored in Chapter 3.

❑ 2.10 Conclusions

It is hard to identify a work role which has changed, and continues to change, as rapidly as that of scheme managers of sheltered housing. Scheme managers not only have to keep up with policy change, they are key players in its delivery. The speed, depth and breadth of the changes are made harder to encompass because scheme managers are members of a dispersed workforce, and have traditionally been somewhat isolated from the mainstream.

There are numerous publications, toolkits and other materials associated with the changing aspects of the role, which can help scheme managers to understand their changing role in greater depth. Useful links and publications can be found in Appendix 1 at the end of this Guide.

The case studies and examples in this chapter show that change has been a positive journey for many scheme managers. But it is a difficult journey to make alone. The importance of regular support for scheme-based staff from their service manager, together with information and training, cannot be over-emphasised. The role of the service manager, together with the key elements of effective service management, are explored in Chapter 6.

CHAPTER 3

WORKING WITH DIVERSITY

Older people are an extremely diverse group. However, this diversity has not previously been reflected throughout sheltered housing. Providers now need to focus on meeting the needs of a more diverse range of clients, ensuring that sheltered housing is accessible to all.

For providers that have only recently begun to focus on diversity in sheltered housing, this chapter raises key points to consider. As the older black and minority ethnic population increases, providers should ensure their services meet cultural and religious needs as well as the support needs of these groups. Equally, providers must recognise that diversity goes beyond race, culture and ethnicity, and applies to issues such as sexuality, as well as to sensory impairments, dementia and other forms of mental illness, learning disability, homelessness and substance abuse.

The chapter also explores the potential of the mobility schemes and choice-based lettings systems that are now in operation across the UK, which publicise vacancies within sheltered housing to an increasingly diverse range of older people.

❑ 3.1 Working with black and minority ethnic (BME) older people

There has been a growing recognition, for example in the Housing Corporation's *Strategy for Older People* (2003), that while health-related needs have been addressed by providers for some time, there has been less recognition of racial and cultural diversity, with the result that it is difficult for some older BME people to access suitable sheltered housing and take up services. Providers are urged to find out more about older BME people's needs and preferences, and to work with this client group to provide appropriate services to meet likely demand in the future.

Sheltered housing providers are addressing these issues in a range of ways:

- Some providers are working towards encouraging BME older people to take up places in existing schemes where currently few or no residents are from BME backgrounds.
- Some providers are developing new schemes, in partnership with local support groups for BME older people, in which the service users and on-site staff reflect the ethnic mix in the local community, and where culturally sensitive services are delivered.
- Specialist BME associations already offer, and are continuing to develop services which target the specific linguistic, cultural and religious needs of existing and potential service users.

Planning for diversity needs to take place at both a strategic and operational level. Creating and maintaining relevant local links is vital, and a crucial starting point is to make contact with older people from BME communities to obtain their views about existing sheltered housing schemes and to identify the barriers to accessing these. From this, providers can work with them to look at ways of redesigning services to meet their needs and aspirations.

■ Encouraging BME older people to take up places in existing schemes

A very gradual approach is needed, and the first task is to critically evaluate the service from the perspective of older BME people, ensuring that existing provision can be adjusted to meet a range of needs. Steps must be taken to make the environment welcoming for BME older people, by offering genuinely responsive services such as access to translation and interpretation, arrangements for religious observance, or accommodating specific dietary needs.

The next stage is to work with local BME community support groups to make links with older people who might be interested in taking up places on the scheme. As sheltered housing is a relatively unknown concept within many BME groups, it can be helpful to use the general information leaflets and audio-tapes produced by ERoSH, as they introduce the concept of sheltered housing in a range of community languages. At the same time, providers can raise awareness of local sheltered housing schemes, using literature printed in relevant community languages, and using appropriate imagery.

Providers also need to consult with existing residents about the steps being taken to widen the range of people being housed. The organisation must be prepared to manage any resistance that may exist amongst existing residents. Following this process, older members of BME groups can be invited to visit open days, coffee mornings etc taking place at local schemes in order to better understand what sheltered housing is, and what it can offer them. The participation of local BME support groups is vital at all stages in the development of such initiatives. Their support will be particularly valuable where the provider is not currently associated with BME provision.

Swaythling Housing Society

Swaythling has taken positive steps to build relations with the older Asian community in Southampton by organising exchange visits between sheltered scheme residents and members of Roshni, a social group for Asian elders.

The visits have been very successful, and the older people involved have been glad of the opportunity to get to know each other better. At one visit everyone discussed their experiences of ageing. This approach, which transcends race and culture, highlighted people's common experiences, both good (for example are people more respected when they are older?) and bad (for example health problems, need for adaptations, isolation) and encouraged conversation about how things could be improved.

Positive outcomes include:

- Breaking down barriers and contributing to community cohesion, including setting an example to children and grandchildren
- Publicising Swaythling's sheltered schemes to the local BME community
- Current scheme residents more likely to welcome future residents from the BME community.

Building on the success of the initiative, Southampton Voluntary Service has granted funding for further joint social activities.

Hanover Housing Association

One of Hanover's schemes in Nottingham was located in an area with a relatively large Chinese population. Through the efforts of the scheme manager and her colleagues, the number of Chinese residents at the 60-property scheme has increased from three to nine. Specific steps included:

- Creating stronger links with the local Chinese population, and with the Chinese Welfare Association, a voluntary community group
- Using Babel, an internet-based translation service, to pass on messages to Chinese residents. Babel is free, and while only a maximum of 150 words can be translated at any one time, it is ideal for short messages
- Producing an illustrated leaflet aimed at Chinese elders who want to find out more about the scheme. One side is in English and the other is in Cantonese
- Encouraging prospective Chinese residents to attend scheme open days
- Using Hanover's central Tenant Participation Fund to hire a translator from the Chinese Welfare Association, for example to help at open days and to assist with making Support Plans.

■ Developing new schemes

Schemes which are developed to meet the needs of particular BME communities require close links with relevant BME community groups to ensure that the location and design, as well as the management of the scheme, will be appropriate for this client group. For non-specialist providers in particular, it is imperative to work with relevant cultural associations and groups when developing the scheme. On-site staff usually reflect the predominant cultural or ethnic group(s) whose needs the provider aims to meet.

Whoever develops the scheme, links with wider partners from the statutory and voluntary sectors are equally important in ensuring diverse needs are met, as the next case study clearly illustrates.

Methodist Homes Housing Association

Bradley Court, an Extra Care sheltered housing scheme in Huddersfield, was developed through a partnership between Methodist Homes Housing Association (MHHA), Kirklees Black Elders Association and Kirklees Metropolitan Council. The scheme has 46 flats and extensive communal facilities and gardens.

Kirklees Black Elders Association is a well established agency which supports older black people in a variety of ways including providing day care centres, lunch clubs and domiciliary care. They identified that many of their clients were living in unsuitable properties, and would benefit from accommodation specifically designed to meet the needs of older people which could also offer a range of additional services such as on-site care and support, culturally appropriate meals, access to social opportunities and access to visiting services such as chiropody, occupational therapy and district nursing. They approached MHHA, which has expertise in both the design and development of older people's housing and of delivering care, and the two organisations formed a partnership, based on shared values and aspirations, with a view to jointly developing such a scheme. Kirklees Metropolitan Council supported the project from the start, as it fitted well into the local older people's housing strategy and with the council's commitment to develop services specifically for the black community.

MHHA provides the housing and facilities management at the scheme. Kirklees Black Elders Association employs an on-site care team which provides a 24-hour care service. Catering services at the scheme are provided by a local small business which offers meals both in the scheme and to other local groups. Both European and West Indian menus are available on a daily basis.

→

The project aims to ensure that at least 50% of the people living at Bradley Court are from the African Caribbean Community. Culturally sensitive care services are provided across the scheme, along with culturally appropriate supporting services such as hairdressing, catering and social activities. The care team at Bradley Court, employed by Kirklees Black Elders Association, reflects the make-up of the tenant population, as do the on-site housing management staff employed by MHHA.

A day centre for local older people, adjoining the scheme, is currently under construction by MHHA, in partnership with Age Concern Kirklees, which successfully fundraised the capital. The day centre will provide care for a further 60 local older people and offer a range of additional services to the community, including evening classes, social opportunities, access to training employment and volunteering.

Family Housing Association (Wales)

Swan Gardens is an innovative sheltered housing scheme for older Chinese people, developed by Family Housing Association (Wales). A unique feature of the scheme is the fact that almost none of the tenants are able to understand, read or speak English.

It was therefore vital that scheme staff should be fluent in both English and Cantonese, in order to support tenants. It was also essential to provide pre-tenancy support to everyone who had expressed an interest in living at this scheme, to help them complete their applications, discuss any support needs they may have and identify what additional help they might need in accessing benefits etc.

This pre-tenancy work was seen as indispensable, as many prospective tenants were completely reliant on family carers, with no independent income, and in some cases not even basic furniture of their own.

The team is fluent in Cantonese, Hakka, Mandarin and English. Recruited five months ahead of the projected opening of the scheme, one project worker was able to carry out interviewing, liaison and other essential work on behalf of the prospective tenants.

Salary during this pre-tenancy period was partly funded by a HACT grant, since there was no Supporting People income at that time to cover staff costs.

→

Once the scheme was opened, further in-depth work was carried out with individual residents. A number of challenges were encountered:

- Linguistic barriers
- Dispersed community
- Disability and health issues
- Reliance on family carers
- Lack of knowledge about service provision
- Lack of culturally appropriate services
- Poverty
- Social isolation.

Overwhelmingly, linguistic barriers remain the main challenge both to service provision at Swan Gardens, and to the ability of Swan Gardens' tenants to lead independent lives. A great deal of work is planned around events and activities to expand the integration of the Swan Gardens tenants into the wider local community.

■ BME providers

Specialist BME providers have a head start in terms of understanding the linguistic, cultural and religious needs of the client groups they were set up to meet. However, changes in the population of a particular area can mean that they too need to form partnerships in order to provide services for a wider range of service users, as the following case study shows.

United Housing Association

Roshni Ghar is a sheltered scheme, originally designed for Asian elders in inner city Bristol. As housing needs have fluctuated within the local community, Roshni Ghar has become a multicultural scheme, offering accommodation to Asian, Somali, Chinese and African Caribbean residents. The scheme co-ordinator is fluent in several Asian languages and holds regular meetings with an interpreter for the Chinese and Somali residents.

United HA works closely with a range of local cultural community groups, both to publicise voids and ensure residents receive signposting to culturally appropriate co-ordinated support.

By offering a range of activity classes, basic English classes and a variety of culturally driven social events, communication and cultural barriers have been broken down.

→

Residents have embraced the diversity within the scheme, and there is a real sense of neighbourliness despite the language difficulties.

United HA has made significant efforts to involve residents in the management and promotion of Roshni Ghar. Residents have helped with stalls at external publicity events; they assist the scheme co-ordinator with scheme inspections; two residents sat on the interview panel to recruit the new scheme co-ordinator, and most residents have attended a recent series of focus meetings to look at service delivery in a range of areas.

BME providers possess invaluable experience in terms of offering specialist services to particular client groups. Contracting and partnership arrangements between BME associations and non-specialist providers can allow this expertise to be shared in order to benefit greater numbers of BME clients, as illustrated in the following case study.

ASRA Midlands

ASRA Midlands HA operates a 24-hour call centre which provides emergency services to residents at all of its sheltered housing schemes across the East and West Midlands. The service offers an immediate response and reassurance service to residents, using the latest monitoring equipment. All control centre staff can communicate in the principal Asian languages, and are sensitive to the linguistic, cultural, and religious requirements of service users.

ASRA also provides this service to other housing organisations, including Derwent Living's Rawdon Street sheltered housing scheme which was remodelled two years ago to meet the needs of Asian elders. The scheme now houses a very diverse community, in which residents speak Punjabi, Hindi and Urdu as their first languages. Derwent Living wanted to provide a control centre service with bilingual staff who could communicate effectively with, and be culturally sensitive to the needs of people from the Asian community, so they turned to ASRA Midlands as a specialist provider.

During the process of setting up this arrangement, the Rawdon Street residents were encouraged to visit ASRA Midlands to meet the staff and see the control centre. Residents expressed their appreciation of the service, particularly of the respectful way ASRA staff spoke to them, and stressed that it helped them feel safe and happy at home.

Good practice checklist: Working with BME older people

- ✓ Make links with local BME support groups
- ✓ Publicise sheltered housing and its benefits in relevant community languages/journals
- ✓ Invite older members of BME groups to informal events on schemes
- ✓ Work with partner agencies in the statutory and voluntary sectors to ensure the services delivered can meet culturally diverse needs
- ✓ Ensure a relevant translation service is readily available
- ✓ When setting up a new scheme for members of a particular ethnic community, ensure the scheme manager can communicate easily with residents
- ✓ Offer or organise a peripatetic warden service across the area using staff with language skills
- ✓ Recruit from BME communities for scheme manager posts
- ✓ Recognise that pre-tenancy support, translation and interpretation services are key aspects of setting up and maintaining a successful service
- ✓ Look at scheme design – eg two bedroom homes (more popular not just with older people from BME communities, but in general)
- ✓ Take all opportunities to celebrate cultural diversity within sheltered housing schemes
- ✓ Ensure scheme managers have ongoing training and support on cultural and diversity issues.

Where cultural and ethnic diversity already exists within an organisation, it is important to take every opportunity to celebrate it. Central and Cecil Housing Trust operates in some of the most culturally and ethnically diverse areas of London:

Central and Cecil Housing Trust

Central and Cecil celebrated diversity at one of their sheltered housing schemes in Camden. The one-day event was a festival of dance and music from around the world, aimed at highlighting the diversity of cultures and backgrounds of Central and Cecil's residents and staff. A series of different performances and practical dance workshops took place throughout the day including flamenco, salsa, ballroom dancing and a steel band. Attendees included residents and staff from several of Central and Cecil's sheltered schemes, and there are plans to repeat this successful event.

❑ 3.2 Working with older lesbians and gay men

At least two London Boroughs' Supporting People strategies quote research published by Polari in 1995 which concluded that the vast majority of older lesbians and gay men would value living in accommodation which met their needs but that most have little confidence in existing accommodation. The study found that there was a lack of understanding among many providers of older people's services on the issues of sexuality and the lifestyles of older lesbians and gay men. A more recent research study, by Opening Doors in Thanet, came to very similar conclusions. In Scotland, research carried out by ODS identified that many older lesbian, gay, bisexual and transgender (LGBT) people were concerned about the kind of housing and support services which might be available to them as they aged. To raise awareness of these issues Communities Scotland has published a booklet *Housing Options for Older LGBT People in Scotland*.

Since 2002 Polari, a gay-managed organisation, has been working with older lesbians, gay men, bisexuals, service providers and commissioners in three London boroughs and is currently developing good practice and awareness points, summarised in the checklist below.

Good practice checklist: Working with older lesbians, gay men and bisexuals (LGB)

Frontline staff should:

- ✓ Assume that some residents/applicants will be LGB even if not identified
- ✓ Take extra care with confidentiality, including with contractors
- ✓ Be aware that homophobia and hate crime affects people of all ages and comes from people of all ages
- ✓ Understand the law on hate crime and know it often falls into a gap between the police and landlords.

Service managers should:

- ✓ Recognise and share existing good practice
- ✓ Ensure that staff have training on sexuality and older people, including on the needs of LGBs
- ✓ Ensure that LGB-friendly statements are prominent in publicity
- ✓ Address allocations procedures to relieve the possible isolation of older LGBs and to offer housing in areas they find more LGB-friendly
- ✓ Have strategies to deal with homophobic behaviour from other service users (or staff) with clear guidelines and organisational support at all levels
- ✓ Know existing and forthcoming law on succession, assignment and same sex partners
- ✓ Seek advice on monitoring the numbers of older LGBs.

Checklist based on information compiled by Polari.

❑ 3.3 Working with service users with a sensory impairment

Service users with a hearing or sight impairment have a range of diverse needs to which the provider and the scheme manager must respond sensitively, and which may require specific action in order to ensure the service user is fully involved in community life. Specially adapted community alarms, doorbells with flashing lights, loop systems in the communal areas, scheme and organisational literature presented in formats such as large print, Braille or on tape are all ways for providers to ensure an inclusive approach.

Scheme managers should build up a knowledge of the resources available from local and national support groups such as the RNIB and RNID, and should receive specific training on effective communication with this client group. For example, some scheme managers complete deaf awareness and British Sign Language courses in order to communicate more effectively with particular residents and reduce their isolation.

❑ 3.4 Working with service users with dementia and other forms of mental illness

It is well established that the incidence of dementia increases significantly with age. After the age of 85, the likelihood of developing some form of dementia rises to 22%. A 1995 report estimated that there is an average of three people with dementia in each sheltered housing scheme in the UK. A recent Fact Sheet for the Department of Health *Extra Care Housing Options for Older People with Functional Mental Health Problems* highlighted the range of mental health problems, in addition to dementia, such as depression, anxiety and schizophrenia, that can affect older people.

In order that the increasing numbers of older people with dementia and cognitive impairments within sheltered housing can be properly supported, scheme managers themselves must be well supported and trained. In particular, they need to:

- Know how to deal effectively and sensitively with people with dementia and cognitive impairments
- Understand how to deal with risk while promoting independence
- Be able to work with service users as individuals in a person-centred way
- Encourage inclusivity across the scheme
- Know how to access help for service users from specialist groups or statutory agencies.

These are specialist areas, and the training and support offered must reflect this.

Furthermore, scheme managers are affected by the impact of such service users on the rest of the scheme, and need regular and ongoing support in working with other residents, who may be negative or critical of older people with dementia and cognitive impairments living on the scheme. Providers need to be aware of the implications of the increasing numbers of sheltered housing residents with dementia and other forms of mental illness, and take proactive steps to ensure that this is managed appropriately.

Housing 21

In response to the challenges faced by scheme managers supporting a growing number of sheltered housing tenants with mild cognitive impairments and dementia, Housing 21 appointed a dementia services adviser.

The adviser offers:

- Professional advice and support to scheme managers in how to access services from the statutory agencies, involving the tenant and/or their carer wherever possible
- Crisis support (for example preventing inappropriate admission to hospital and/or residential care)
- Policy and good practice guidelines on working with tenants and their carers during the early stages of dementia
- Help for the scheme manager in identifying the difference between suspected dementia, and depression (offering information and advice on good practice in person-centred dementia care)
- Support for scheme managers in knowing when to intervene with tenants at risk of harm either to themselves (eg self-neglect) or other tenants, and supporting them in taking action
- A telephone advice service in office hours
- Work with tenants, when they want advice and support in supporting fellow tenants whom they know or suspect may have dementia.

Other activities include a training programme on dementia awareness, advice on the design of new buildings, support for home care staff and work on using assistive technologies. The post also promotes good practice based on Housing 21's work in dementia care.

The postholder is professionally mentored by Dementia Voice, part of Housing 21's group structure.

The development of specific sheltered and retirement schemes for service users with dementia is a relatively recent initiative. There are some particularly innovative examples of this provision within the leasehold sector, as shown in the example below.

Methodist Homes for the Aged

Fitzwarren Court in Swindon is a leasehold extra care housing project which has been developed by the charity Methodist Homes for the Aged (MHA). It comprises 14 one and two bedroom apartments which are offered on a leasehold for sale basis to older people where one partner is living with dementia, thus enabling couples to remain together.

A specialist dementia care service is delivered within the scheme by MHA, which has pioneered work in this field across a range of provision. The flats are close to a dementia nursing home built by MHA at the same time as the flats, and services such as catering, laundry and cleaning are provided from the home. A range of assistive technology is available to residents of the flats, and care is provided by a dedicated team registered as a domiciliary care agency.

Assistive technology and dementia care

The following case studies show the great potential of assistive technology to support particularly frail older people, including those with dementia.

Maidstone Housing Trust

In partnership with social services and Tunstall Telecom, Maidstone Housing Trust has developed and fully equipped a Smart Home displaying all the latest assistive technology. The equipment available includes fall detectors, gas shut-off valves, flood detectors and movement pads which can also switch on lights etc. This home is available for any interested person to visit, from partner agencies to families with relatives who have the onset of dementia, and users themselves.

One of Maidstone's sheltered scheme co-ordinators is a lead officer for dementia, and attends local meetings to stay abreast of new aids and services.

Methodist Homes Housing Association

Methodist Homes Housing Association (MHHA) uses a range of assistive technology as part of a programme for supporting clients with dementia, and is currently assessing the effectiveness of technological products in order to 'future-proof' new developments.

→

The 'Vivatec Wristcare' system is being evaluated within one extra care housing scheme which has 20 flats for older people living with dementia. Some scheme residents have volunteered to pilot the wristband, which monitors the user's health and wellbeing on a 24-hour basis with minimal intrusion, in order to reduce the risks a user faces, and provides information about their needs. It can trigger an automatic alarm when the device is removed, or if the user appears unconscious.

MHHA have appointed Dementia North to evaluate the scheme and the assistive technology in its first year of operation and to undertake a dementia mapping exercise with all tenants at the scheme over the next three years to identify improvements to their wellbeing as a result of receiving specialist dementia care at the scheme.

❑ 3.5 Working with service users with learning disabilities

Some providers have housed people with moderate or mild learning disabilities in sheltered schemes. Contrary to some negative perceptions, if this is managed effectively it can work well, not only for the service user but for the scheme as a whole. Those with learning disabilities can have a lot to offer and be a positive strength in the sheltered community. For service users, the benefits of the security, companionship and community elements that sheltered housing offers can give them confidence to grow and develop independent living skills, particularly for those with previous bad experiences of living in the wider community.

StepForward

A successful case study from StepForward shows how two men with learning disabilities (J and D) achieved a better quality of life through moving into sheltered housing in their 40s.

J and D had shared a house, with specialist learning disability support, for many years. However, there were concerns about their unequal relationship and the extent to which J took all the decisions while D deferred to him, despite extensive work to challenge the problem. A series of burglaries prompted J and D to look for a safer environment, and although StepForward was unable to locate any suitable accommodation for them to share, there were two separate flats available in a sheltered scheme in J and D's preferred area.

→

J and D accepted the offer of the flats, where the continuing specialist support was to be complemented by the support service from the sheltered scheme manager. Both settled well into their new surroundings, engage fully in the community life on offer, and are accepted by their neighbours. This was the first time D had lived on his own, and he needed a lot of support. However, his confidence has developed to the point where he joins in all the social activities at the scheme, no longer 'seeks permission' from J, manages his own money, and does his own cooking and shopping with support.

Good practice checklist: Integrating people with learning disabilities into sheltered housing

- ✓ Ensure clear criteria for eligibility and avoid restrictive criteria based on age
- ✓ Hold a robust multi-disciplinary assessment and support planning meeting, prior to letting, involving the scheme manager, the prospective tenant, their family and friends, and external agencies
- ✓ Define clearly in a contract the support to be provided, and agree on an action plan for contingencies
- ✓ House the tenant in their own local area wherever possible
- ✓ Ensure ongoing input from a named social worker who communicates regularly with the scheme manager
- ✓ Anticipate initial resistance from some staff and residents to the introduction of people with learning disabilities – listen to and allay fears and concerns – go beyond labels and explode myths.

See also the general good practice checklist on page 63 on working with a range of vulnerable clients.

❑ 3.6 Resettling older homeless people into sheltered housing

Use of sheltered housing to house older homeless people is becoming more common. In some cases this is more by default than design, and is regarded by the provider as a way of filling voids in hard-to-let schemes. However, other providers, such as Focus Futures, Thames Reach/Bondway and the Sir Oswald Stoll Foundation have built or designated certain schemes or flats particularly for this group, and have trained staff to work with such service users, in response to a growing need.

Evidence shows that these service users need clearly defined support to resettle into permanent accommodation, particularly where substance abuse and/or mental health issues associated with their previous circumstances can lead to challenging behaviour. Problems inevitably ensue where allocations to this client group are made within mainstream schemes without clear planning, robust support systems in place, and training and support for the scheme manager.

Such service users are frequently resented by the more 'traditional' residents, and without proper support systems in place which take account of the specific needs of this group, their rehabilitation is unlikely to be achieved. Thus, while such allocations may solve a voids problem in the short term, in the longer term this approach can lead to management problems for the provider.

However, where good support is available, such initiatives can offer a rehabilitative environment which enables clients to reach their potential, as the case study from Focus Futures shows.

Focus Futures

St Eugene's Court in Birmingham provides 44 self-contained flats and communal areas for older Irish men who have experienced social exclusion and have additional support needs around their health, living skills or alcohol use. The project was set up as a partnership by Focus Futures and Irish Welfare and Advice Service. The client group was consulted on the design, and the building is bright, open and spacious with good quality furniture and fittings.

In addition to providing supported housing the scheme also houses a drop-in centre which enables up to 40 additional people a day from a similar client group to have a nutritious meal, company and activities. The drop-in centre adds to the project's sense of being integrated into the community, having a dynamic atmosphere and providing a sense of belonging.

Supporting People funding for the project is £107 per client, per week. Each client's support package is co-ordinated by an in-house staff team which delivers it along with statutory and voluntary agencies such as mental health teams, alcohol services, probation services and primary care teams. Some tenants require care as well as support, which is delivered by outside care companies in conjunction with social services and the tenants themselves.

Good practice checklist: Effective resettlement of older homeless people into sheltered housing

- ✓ Ensure a thorough assessment before the tenancy – focus on social isolation, risk assessment, mental health, previous housing history
- ✓ Hold a risk assessment and support planning meeting, prior to letting, involving the scheme manager, the prospective tenant, their family and friends, and external agencies
- ✓ Define clearly in a contract the support to be provided and agree on an action plan for contingencies
- ✓ Ensure ongoing input from a resettlement worker who communicates regularly with the scheme manager
- ✓ Provide training, resources and ongoing support for scheme managers on alcohol, mental health, learning disability, offending behaviour and homelessness issues
- ✓ Ensure alcohol sensitive home care is available when necessary.

Help the Aged and HACT funded research into this issue in Manchester, and this checklist is adapted from that work. Readers are encouraged to read the full report *Sheltered housing and the resettlement of older homeless people* (2002).

See also the general good practice checklist on page 63 on working with a range of vulnerable clients.

❑ 3.7 Working with older people with alcohol and drug dependency

Misuse of drugs and alcohol is increasing in the population as a whole, and this is reflected in sheltered and retirement housing. The consequences of alcohol misuse in sheltered housing can range from minimal effect on others to violence and aggression towards other residents and staff, and damage to property.

Within sheltered accommodation it is essential to reduce the impact on the individual, other residents, and the community and therefore a resident who is behaving in an anti-social manner must be challenged and helped to address their alcohol consumption. One of the most successful methods of tackling alcohol misuse is to develop harm minimisation strategies that encourage responsible attitudes towards alcohol consumption.

Scheme managers should assess the individual needs of service users and seek to refer them to appropriate local services such as St Mungo's in order to stabilise their behaviour. The priority of staff members is to restrict the impact the client's behaviour has on the community and on their tenancy, therefore early intervention is very important.

Willow Housing

St Mungo's charity had a short-term Supporting People contract to help scheme managers at Willow Housing in Brent to work with alcohol-dependent tenants. This approach was integrated with other measures taken by Willow to address anti-social behaviour in sheltered housing, including the development of a specific policy and multi-agency training on anti-social behaviour in sheltered schemes.

❑ 3.8 Choice-based lettings

Fundamental changes in approaches to promoting and letting social rented housing have brought many benefits for potential sheltered housing residents, but also raise some issues for providers about assessing health and care needs, particularly in relation to Supporting People.

In the original allocation systems used by most local authorities and housing associations to let sheltered housing, local connection was often a key criterion. Older people's accommodation options have been considerably increased by the mobility schemes, choice-based lettings systems, and common housing registers that are now in operation across the UK. While such schemes generally operate common eligibility criteria for sheltered housing, applicants who comply can now bid to move to a new location, perhaps because they want to be nearer to relatives, or for health reasons.

Through publicity relating to these schemes, particularly via the internet, older people, their relatives and carers from a range of different areas, locations and client groups can access information about many vacancies in sheltered housing, the existence of which they may not have previously known about. In this way, the pool of applicants for vacancies within sheltered housing is widening, which in turn creates the potential to enhance the diversity of sheltered housing communities overall.

However, choice-based lettings and common housing registers present challenges to sheltered housing providers within the context of Supporting People. A core principle of Supporting People is partnership working between social services, health, housing and probation to support independence, underpinned by a clear customer focus. As such, there is considerable potential to make connections with choice-based lettings. Nevertheless, there are a number of local implementation issues that need to be addressed. These include ensuring agreement and possibly commonality of criteria and targets. For example, it is important to establish protocols within the lettings process for accommodation that involves health and care assessments while at the same time enabling customers (with help and support) to have choices.

Within the new framework there are considerable opportunities to enable vulnerable people to be made more fully aware of the wide range of heath, care and housing opportunities that exist. Choice-based lettings publicity can be used to publicise options such as care and repair and disabled facilities grants, as well as the existence of sheltered housing.

Evidence from a number of pilots has highlighted that vulnerable households welcome the principle of choice and value the openness and transparency of the new systems. The three key issues in implementing choice are:

- Providing support and advice when and where it is needed
- Ensuring that appropriate information about properties and neighbourhood facilities is readily available
- Achieving greater degrees of collaboration between the wide range of agencies involved in providing services for vulnerable people.

The following two case studies illustrate the diverse ways that sheltered housing providers are adopting choice-based lettings:

Sanctuary Housing

Sanctuary Housing introduced a new lettings policy in 2004 intended to increase customer choice as applicants are provided with more information about waiting times and property types.

Depending on their circumstances, applicants are placed into one of four priority bands in date order. The caring, coping and support needs of applicants, together with medical and social factors are considered alongside their housing need. Designated staff, ideally the scheme manager, undertake and record a needs and risk assessment for sheltered housing applicants. Upon rehousing this information also provides a basis for an initial support plan.

Within each band lettings are made on the basis of date order. The percentage of lettings from each band is determined by regional lettings targets which are set to ensure reasonable preference is given to those in greatest housing need. Within this framework local lettings plans (developed in consultation with local authorities and approved by regional boards) allow Sanctuary's regions to respond sensitively to local issues at a scheme level. For sheltered housing, these plans can be used to set out that applicants in the 'urgent' or 'high' bands will always be prioritised for schemes where support services eligible for Supporting People grant are provided. Alternatively they could be used to establish that lettings to older people with a lower level of need would be temporarily prioritised at a scheme where the support needs of residents exceeded the resources of frontline staff.

Home Connections

Home Connections is a large-scale choice-based lettings scheme which advertises and lets local authority and housing association properties in parts of London and the Midlands. It helps partner organisations to promote their sheltered housing schemes using virtual tours which can be viewed via the internet. These tours, which feature scaled floor plans, 360-degree panoramic photography and voice-activated description, enable older people looking for a sheltered home to find out more about available properties without having to travel.

SPH Housing is one housing association which advertised its sheltered housing more widely by working with the London Borough of Camden and Home Connections.

❑ 3.9 Conclusions

Initiatives to improve diversity within sheltered housing require careful planning and preparation both at a strategic and operational level in order to succeed.

Strategic approaches must take account of the local Supporting People five year strategy and the older people's strategies for the area. In addition, where there is a move towards making sheltered housing allocations to 'non traditional' vulnerable clients, such as younger people with learning disabilities, or formerly homeless older people who may have substance abuse problems, this should be a clear policy decision, rather than by default. A robust relationship with social services and other key agencies and support groups must be developed and maintained to ensure these groups of service users receive the additional support they will need to maintain their tenancies and to reach their potential within this environment.

Providers must be aware of the implications of choice-based lettings systems, which are likely to open up sheltered housing to an increasingly diverse range of service users. Partnerships and protocols must be developed with key local agencies to balance the principles of need and choice.

Scheme managers have a key role to play in terms of creating and maintaining relevant local links and partnerships in order to support vulnerable service users. To succeed, they must be well supported and trained to deal with the extra demands which a more diverse client group will inevitably place upon them.

General good practice checklist: Working with a range of vulnerable service users

Alongside the checklists relating to the needs of the specific groups covered within this chapter, the following good practice points should be adopted when working with an increasingly diverse group within sheltered housing:

- ✓ Monitor the out-of-hours input of resident scheme managers
- ✓ Review the accessibility and transparency of sheltered application processes
- ✓ Sustain tenants' relationships with supportive friends and family wherever possible
- ✓ Help the tenant to attend activities on- or off-site
- ✓ Help the tenant to build good relationships with neighbours in the scheme
- ✓ Avoid housing people with extremely challenging behaviours into mainstream schemes
- ✓ Offer some fully furnished flats
- ✓ Develop partnerships and protocols with key local agencies.

CHAPTER 4

WORKING IN PARTNERSHIP

Partnership working by staff at all levels is essential if older people living in sheltered housing are to be at the centre of service delivery. This chapter looks at the benefits of partnership working for service users and organisations. It examines the strategic opportunities for, and challenges to, working in partnership with other agencies, particularly health and social services, in the context of current programmes and agendas:

- Joint working – the bigger picture
- The division between care and support
- The relationship between Supporting People and community care
- Improving partnership working between sheltered and retirement housing and health and social care agencies
- The relationship between the National Service Framework (NSF) for Older People and sheltered and retirement housing
- Falls, health promotion and healthy living (standards 6 and 8 in the NSF) and the role of sheltered and retirement housing
- Intermediate care (standard 3 in the NSF) and the role of sheltered housing in providing intermediate care settings
- Extra Care.

The chapter also highlights successful partnership work within the sheltered and retirement sector, through the Housing for Older People Alliance, and concludes with some local examples which demonstrate what can be achieved through effective joint working between public and private organisations, sheltered scheme residents and the wider community.

❑ 4.1 Joint working – the bigger picture

Partnership working is frequently quoted and aspired to, but can be very difficult to achieve in practice. More than ever, sheltered housing providers depend on effective partnerships at strategic, operational and practical levels in order to meet residents' needs. Conversely, there is a greater recognition by other agencies that they need to call on sheltered housing in order to meet their own targets.

Successive governments have grappled for decades with the negative consequences of a complex multiplicity of statutory, voluntary and private agencies providing services for older people. The Audit Commission report on community care in 1986 had a chapter whose title eloquently summed up the key problems – "Organisational fragmentation and confusion". Since that time the NHS and Community Care Act 1990 and many other measures have addressed these problems – including:

- Modernising Social Services 1998
- Health and Social Services Act 1999
- National Service Framework for Older People 2001
- National Service Framework for Mental Health 2001
- Public Health White Paper 2004.

At a local level, many sheltered and retirement staff will be familiar with some of the challenges to overcome when trying to make links with health and social care professionals:

- 'Patients' or 'service users/clients' are not necessarily identified by health or social care agencies as living in sheltered housing
- Assessment/discharge planning processes may exclude sheltered housing staff
- Other professionals may be unaware of the changing role or of the potential of scheme managers and sheltered housing
- Other professionals may have negative or out-of-date views of scheme managers
- Other professionals may sometimes use confidentiality as a barrier
- Strategic planning by health and social services may exclude housing.

Despite the legacy of obstacles to joint working (different budgets, priorities, cultures, funding and accountability structures) the current climate actively promotes partnership and provides extensive opportunities for sheltered housing to seek out and be welcomed into partnership arrangements, as subsequent sections of this chapter demonstrate.

Opportunities for sheltered and retirement housing are presented by Supporting People. For decades, housing staff have complained of their invisibility in the wider community care agendas. The origins of ERoSH (and its predecessor, the Emerging Role of the Warden project) lie in the dissatisfaction of frontline sheltered housing staff about their frequent exclusion from case conferences, assessments and hospital discharge planning. The Audit Commission report *Home Alone* and now Supporting People guidance urge health and social services to work together with sheltered housing providers in order to deliver the 'home for life' promise. As ERoSH and previous editions of this Guide have stated, sheltered housing cannot provide older people with a 'home for life' or even quality of life by unilateral declaration – it can only happen as a result of truly joined-up working with housing, health, voluntary and independent sectors and social services at strategic and operational levels. A CIH Scotland publication *Essential Connections: linking housing, health and social care* raises the profile of housing within health and social care partnership agendas in order to improve delivery of services to people with support needs.

The Department of Health has recognised the need for closer partnership working across health and social care economies, including commissioners and providers of housing, care and support. In 2002, it established the Housing Learning and Improvement Network under the Health and Social Care Change Agent Team. Its national and regional presence enables staff from health, housing and social care agencies to meet regularly, promote good practice, share information and make best use of a range of learning resources and tailored support for capacity building purposes. For details see the website www.changeagentteam.org.uk/housing.

Organisations have been urged to move from delivering services in an autonomous and fragmented way to *coordinate* and work in partnership. Current thinking, particularly for those service users with complex needs, is to move beyond co-ordination to *integration*, as shown in the box below.

The continuum of organisational and professional relationships

AUTONOMY	CO-ORDINATION	INTEGRATION
There is no holistic view of user needs; actions and decisions are arrived at independently and without co-ordination.	There is a shared view of user needs; actions and decision making are coordinated.	Fragmentation between providers and autonomous action are minimised. Working practices become transparent. Integration is of greatest benefit to those with complex needs.

Source: *Integrated Working: a guide*, Integrated Care Network, 2004

Sheltered and retirement housing services are a long way from being set at the integration end of this continuum and only the more progressive and innovative providers will have achieved the co-ordination stage. Co-ordination can be at strategic, operational and/or frontline level, on small or grand scales.

The benefits of improved co-ordination include:

- Faster response to identified needs
- Decision-making processes simplified by involving fewer people
- Better use of resources
- Reduced communication failure
- Increased satisfaction with services.

Good practice checklist: Partnership working is most likely to succeed where...

✓ The political climate is favourable
✓ Friction between local authorities, NHS bodies, general practice and the independent sector is minimised
✓ Senior managers and professional leaders are supportive
✓ Overall objectives are clear and realistic
✓ Resources, including staff skills and time, are adequate to the task
✓ The negative impact of continuous change is being minimised
✓ The clash of professional philosophies and language and the risk of professional tribalism are minimised
✓ The right people with the right skills are involved
✓ There is good communication in and between teams and units at all levels
✓ Staff have 'ownership' of the development
✓ Shadowing/mentoring schemes are in place with partner agencies
✓ Regular updating meetings are held with partner agencies
✓ The roles and responsibilities of staff are clear and understood
✓ Management accountability is clearly delineated and professional support routines are in place
✓ Accommodation and IT are shared
✓ Joint training has been provided and team building is supported
✓ Monitoring and evaluation strategies are built in.

Source: *Integrated Working: a guide*, Integrated Care Network, 2004

❑ 4.2 The division between care and support

Drawing the line between what is social care, health care and support is only necessary because of their continued separate funding. In practice, and for service users, it can be difficult to distinguish the boundaries. Statutory *social care* is funded and commissioned by social services and involves personal tasks such as washing, dressing, feeding, toileting. Statutory home-based *health care* is funded and delivered by primary care trusts and involves tasks such as injections, dressings, inserting and removing of catheters.

Health care is provided free of charge, whilst social care is subject to charging. Each local authority with social services responsibilities has a Fair Access to Care Services document, setting out how they assess and charge for social care services. Where an individual's primary needs are for health care beyond that which social services are able to provide under s21 of the National Assistance Act 1948 they may be eligible for fully funded continuing care from the NHS. Each Strategic Health Authority in England has eligibility criteria for continuing care, agreed with their respective NHS and social services organisations.

Housing related support is funded by Supporting People, provided by housing associations and local authority housing departments and involves non-personal care tasks such as advice giving, advocacy, monitoring, liaison, help in establishing social contacts and activities, help in gaining access to other services, help in maintaining the safety and security of the dwelling, supervision and monitoring of health. Increasingly the voluntary and independent sector, eg Older People's Neighbourhood Networks, is taking on some of the above tasks.

❑ 4.3 Partnership with health and social care agencies

In order for progress to be made it is imperative that there is agreement at the highest levels within the partner organisations about the role and contribution of sheltered and retirement housing in achieving an improved quality of life for older people. This will include sustaining independence and a significant contribution to performance improvements in key areas, for example sustainable hospital discharge, reduced accident and emergency admissions among older people and reduced demand for residential care services. The Supporting People Commissioning Bodies established in each local authority area and the five year Supporting People strategies provide an opportunity to formally secure the co-operation of the key partners.

ERoSH has produced detailed checklists for hospital and primary care staff and for social services staff, as a tool to examine and improve the relationship with sheltered housing services. Extracts are shown below, and the full checklists are available free of charge via the ERoSH contact details given in Appendix 1. ERoSH encourages scheme managers and their managers to obtain sufficient copies of these leaflets to pass on to their counterparts in health and social services. Meetings and/or joint training could be requested to address specific checklist questions. In addition, sheltered housing staff should invite health and/or social care professionals to their team meetings and vice versa to discuss some questions. ERoSH will have achieved its aims of promoting partnership working between sheltered housing staff and staff from health and social services if positive responses are achieved to all the questions on the checklists.

Extract from ERoSH checklist for hospital and primary care staff			
Hospital and primary care staff			
	Yes	**No**	**In progress**
1 Does your patient record form specify whether or not the patient lives in sheltered housing?	❑	❑	❑
2 Do you include the scheme manager's name and phone number on the form?	❑	❑	❑
3 Are your staff aware of the range and types of sheltered housing available locally?	❑	❑	❑
4 Have you incorporated an explanation of sheltered housing into staff induction training?	❑	❑	❑
5 Do your local assessment procedures include reference to sheltered housing?	❑	❑	❑
6 Have you discussed with housing providers the rehabilitation potential of sheltered housing (see Standard 3 of the National Service Framework for Older People)?	❑	❑	❑

Extract from ERoSH checklist for social services			
Assessment and care monitoring			
	Yes	**No**	**In progress**
11 Are you confident that the Single Assessment Process in your locality would reveal whether a service user would benefit from sheltered and retirement housing or Extra Care or related support services?	❑	❑	❑
12 Is there a trigger on your assessment forms to ensure that sheltered and retirement housing staff are consulted?	❑	❑	❑
13 Are home care staff aware of what information about a resident is appropriate to be provided to sheltered and retirement housing staff?	❑	❑	❑
14 Have you discussed with sheltered and retirement housing providers the possibility of extending the scheme manager's role to include assessments, key working, monitoring and co-ordinating care delivery?	❑	❑	❑

→

	Yes	No	In progress
15 Do you routinely ask sheltered and retirement housing clients if they would like their scheme manager to be present for the assessment or review?	❑	❑	❑
16 When you are carrying out an assessment or review of a sheltered or retirement housing resident's needs, do you routinely contact the scheme manager beforehand and feed back information after the meeting?	❑	❑	❑
17 Have you explored the use of social alarm systems to monitor the delivery of care?	❑	❑	❑
18 Does your authority have any interim arrangements in the event of older people in hospital needing sheltered housing but unable to return home (eg if the building is unsafe) in the light of the Community Care (Delayed Discharges) Act?	❑	❑	❑
19 Have you considered asking scheme managers to support residents to access Direct Payments?	❑	❑	❑
20 Do you work with other local authorities if an assessment indicates that an older person wants to move to sheltered housing outside their own local authority?	❑	❑	❑

❑ 4.4 Links with the NHS National Service Framework for Older People

The National Service Framework for Older People, one of a series of government NSFs, aims to improve standards of care for older people. Eight national standards and an additional appendix on medicines have been introduced, for the first time setting out national minimum standards for social care. Health authorities, primary care trusts and their colleagues in social services are judged against how they deliver these standards in their local areas – an effective working relationship with housing providers is one of the keys to achieving the standards. A number of the standards are also incorporated into national targets for the NHS and social services departments.

The box opposite, extracted from a leaflet by ERoSH, highlights where sheltered housing can contribute to achieving each standard.

National Service Framework for Older People – making the links with sheltered housing

Standard 1: Rooting out age discrimination

Standard 2: Person-centred care
"Care Trust framework ... should enable housing wardens to be an integral part of the team" (Ch 2 para 2.24)
"The single assessment process should be designed to identify all of their needs" (Ch 2 para 2.29)

Standard 3: Intermediate care
"(options to support people include) ... very sheltered housing" (Ch 2 para 3.14)
"Health and social services should routinely identify the scope for rehabilitation and consider, along with housing authorities, possible alternatives to residential accommodation" (Ch2 para 3.24)

Standard 4: General hospital care
"discharge planning should include ... community support and housing. Arrangements should have been made to ensure that support is in place before discharge home" (Ch 2 para 4.30)

Standard 5: Stroke
"(long term support for stroke patients) should ensure that accommodation after discharge – whether ordinary housing, sheltered housing or a care home – is suitable to meet individual needs and that adaptations and community equipment are provided where appropriate" (Ch 2 para 5.8)

Standard 6: Falls
Nothing specific on sheltered housing but several references to safety in the home and the need for adaptations

Standard 7: Mental health in older people
"(specialist mental health teams for older people) should have agreed working and referral arrangements with ... housing workers" (Ch 2 para 7.48)

Standard 8: The promotion of health and active life in old age
"(agencies working in partnership should) develop healthy communities to support older people to live lives that are as fulfilling as possible" (Ch 2 para 8.2)

Good practice checklist: A planned approach to making links with health professionals

- ✓ 'Brainstorm' with staff/colleagues on what are current local concerns regarding links with health colleagues, and decide who could take forward each issue
- ✓ Include users in this brainstorming and decide with them which are the local priorities for joint work
- ✓ Use the ERoSH Awareness Week to invite health professionals into schemes and promote the rehabilitative and preventive potential of sheltered housing
- ✓ Put the NSF onto the agenda in internal meetings, to raise awareness up and down the organisation
- ✓ Confirm actions agreed with staff at meetings – minutes, key tasks in appraisals, follow up
- ✓ Use the Department of Health website for information on health structures and strategies: www.dh.gov.uk Also see *Briefing paper on NSF for older people and the implications for housing organisations* at www.peterfletcherassociates.co.uk
- ✓ Set up meetings with appropriate health and social services staff, quoting from the NSF as appropriate and using agreed aspects of the checklists in the new ERoSH health leaflet as the agenda
- ✓ Use the most appropriate level internally to talk to the most appropriate level externally
- ✓ Ask senior managers to take problems up on your behalf where a 'Berlin wall' operates between housing staff and other agencies
- ✓ Aim high when approaching other agencies – eg approach the Chair of the primary care trust
- ✓ Contact the local Intermediate Care coordinator – all health authorities must have a designated Intermediate Care coordinator
- ✓ Offer facilities when making your approach, not just a list of problems – eg sheltered housing schemes as a venue for health checks or stroke clubs, involvement of sheltered housing staff in single assessment pilots
- ✓ Build on small successes – eg changing the patient form to include *"is the patient in sheltered housing?"*

Key messages for health professionals about the role of sheltered housing and its staff

- Sheltered housing offers older people a 'home for life', independence, security, company, privacy, own front door, choice, healthy active life
- These aims are achievable only through the right health and social care services being delivered
- Scheme managers are often the only professionals who see tenants every day in their own home – who pick up on sudden or gradual changes in physical or mental health/wellbeing

→

- Scheme managers could be invited to share their assessments, be involved in hospital discharge planning and case conferences
- Scheme managers can monitor the quality and quantity of care packages, referring back to social services and/or health in the event of deficiencies
- Scheme managers can act as advocates for tenants, especially those with no families
- Sheltered housing could offer venues for rehabilitation classes or dedicated flats for Intermediate Care on block contracts to the health trust – to aid early discharge, to prevent hospital admission, to provide rehabilitation.

Twin Valley Homes

Twin Valley Homes worked in partnership with the local primary care trust to map hospital admissions from sheltered housing. The exercise identified lack of understanding by hospital staff of the role of sheltered staff and consequent lack of involvement by sheltered housing staff in hospital discharge planning. Joint training and hospital admission forms were introduced to address these issues.

Single assessments

Standard 2 of the NSF identifies the need for single assessments by health and social services professionals. Some organisations have addressed the potential for duplication with the requirement under Supporting People for a separate Needs and Risk Assessment and Support Plan under the Quality Assessment Framework:

- **The London Borough of Sutton** has included the Single Assessment Contact and Referral form as part of the Support Plan.
- **Guildford Borough Council** bases its needs assessment of prospective and current sheltered housing tenants on the Basic Personal Information (BPI), Contact and Overview Assessment parts of the Single Assessment Process. This will help to inform and strengthen the information gathered in respect of support plans as part of the support planning process. In addition the information on the tenant database is being reviewed to reflect the key themes of the BPI and Contact Assessment.
- **Twin Valley Homes** has taken part in a pilot under the Cumbria and Lancashire NHS Strategic Health Authority focusing on Single Assessment, hospital discharge and care pathways.

Each of these three organisations report improved mutual understanding of roles and responsibilities by health, social services and housing.

❑ 4.5 Falls prevention, health promotion and healthy living

Long-standing frustrations about the lack of partnership working between health and sheltered housing professionals have been overcome by organisations that have seized on the opportunities presented by Standards 6 and 8 in the NSF. The major cause of admissions of older people to hospital is falls, most of which are preventable. Health professionals have to meet clear targets on falls prevention and the promotion of healthy living among older people, and are invariably very receptive to approaches (and offers of venues) from sheltered housing providers.

For example, several organisations have worked with local PCT Falls Co-ordinators addressing Standard 6 in the NSF to arrange presentations to sheltered housing tenants on the prevention of falls, and chair-based Tai Chi exercise classes – maintaining muscle strength, balance and co-ordination to improve mobility and reduce the risk of falls.

Some organisations have set falls prevention as an objective for their scheme managers. Similarly, falls prevention has been incorporated into support plan discussions to identify potential hazards and risks within the home. Initial assessments and referrals to the Falls Co-ordinator are encouraged.

Salford City Council

The 'Sure Footed in Salford' project secured government funding of £100,000 and was partly used to train mobile wardens to identify people at risk of falling due to personal health or hazards in the home. Housing staff are working with partners in health, ambulance, social care and support services to agree how the information is collected and how it can be passed on – to ensure the person at risk receives the right sort of help – both to prevent and treat falls. A directory of older people's services is being compiled. Falls detectors are being trialled and the whole project is currently under evaluation by Bristol University for the ODPM.

There have been many spin-off benefits including:

- The support of housing association colleagues, to extend the training to all wardens in sheltered housing schemes in the city
- Firm plans to remodel areas within sheltered housing schemes to serve as health consulting areas for osteoporosis screening, with plans to resource health staff to be on site, eg GP health checks
- Linking with lifelong learning and leisure services to bring new services into sheltered housing to promote health and wellbeing.

→

The illustration below shows the web of partnerships involved:

- Supporting People commissioning the Care on Call mobile warden service through their employing organisation, New Prospect Housing Ltd
- Care on Call have established relationships with technology providers who supply community alarms and other technology
- Supporting People service commissioning priorities are decided by the City Council and health services
- Supporting People has been key to linking housing services to health and care objectives.

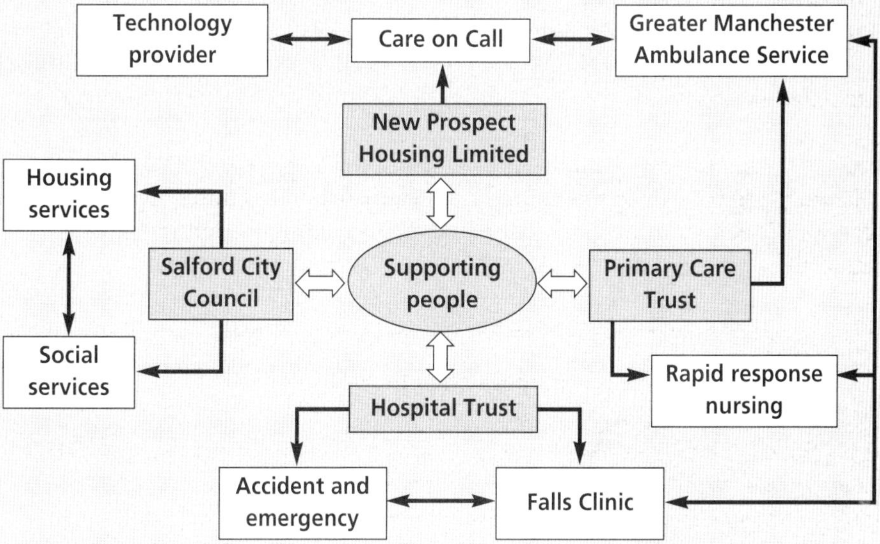

Reducing waiting lists for occupational therapist assessments

Several organisations have taken steps to reduce long waiting lists for occupational therapist assessments, for example:

- **Peterborough City Council**: Occupational therapists working for Adult Social Care train sheltered housing staff to perform low level assessments for grab rails and stair rails, freeing up time for qualified occupational therapists to concentrate on more complex assessments.
- **Selby District Council** trains sheltered housing staff to assess and install simple adaptations for bathing.
- **Manchester City Council** recruits and trains non-occupational therapists to provide lower level assessments – many new staff were previously wardens/scheme managers.

In addition to taking part in specific initiatives, providers should raise awareness of the health and social care benefits enjoyed by sheltered housing residents living in safe, purpose-built accommodation. Recent research into the profile of private sheltered residents showed that they required fewer stays in hospital or GP appointments compared with the general older population. Living in a ready-made community can also help combat loneliness and depression.

❑ 4.6 Intermediate Care

Sheltered housing flats or bedsits are often ideal for Intermediate Care as settings to help prevent inappropriate admissions to hospital and help early discharge, thereby helping to address Standard 3 of the NSF.

An example of how this can work is for the local PCT or social services to lease a small number of units (often otherwise hard-to-let) in a scheme from the landlord. Patients who would otherwise need hospital admission or who need additional support before returning home after a hospital stay are assessed for Intermediate Care. If their needs can be met they are admitted to an Intermediate Care bed for up to six weeks. Typically, dedicated support and care staff are available, along with social work, community nursing, assistive technology and therapy.

Intermediate Care costs are considerably cheaper than in-patient hospital care. In addition social services may be fined £100 per day for any patient medically fit for discharge, but needing social care support. There is therefore a financial incentive for social services to work with housing providers to increase Intermediate Care provision.

Eligibility criteria for Intermediate Care usually include:

- People who need complex adaptations to their home, which could take up to six weeks to be completed
- People who need physical or social rehabilitation, to build their confidence and independence skills, often occupational and/or physiotherapy following a stroke
- People who have a temporary inability to manage at home – for example patients recovering from a fracture and unable to manage the stairs
- People whose needs have changed and who require a multi-disciplinary assessment of their future need for housing, care and support.

The following people are usually excluded:

- Those with severe and enduring mental health problems
- Those with known MRSA
- Those whose condition is medically unstable
- Individuals who are unwilling to engage in a rehabilitation plan.

Good practice checklist: Intermediate Care

- ✓ Set clear objectives but avoid over-rigid contracts and over-complex billing arrangements
- ✓ Devise a mutually-agreed project plan prior to opening the service
- ✓ Joint planning and commissioning between PCTs and social services
- ✓ Agreed admission criteria
- ✓ Anticipate and deal sensitively with concerns by permanent residents such as "turning this place into a nursing home" – acknowledge concerns about transient service users and unknown visitors, and point out likely benefits to them such as presence of on-site care, and future lettings to satisfied patients
- ✓ Ensure positive attitude by scheme managers and flexibility between partner agencies
- ✓ Ensure the support of GPs and hospital discharge teams
- ✓ Formalise an agreement of the services to be provided by social services and health and clearly define the support role of the scheme manager
- ✓ Clarify the different agencies' roles in providing an out-of-hours service and response
- ✓ Choose wheelchair accessible units in schemes with lifts
- ✓ Devise and publicise Plain English leaflets, with photographs, for prospective patients, to explain the purpose of Intermediate Care and to describe the accommodation
- ✓ Ensure that a full explanation of the service is shared with and understood by the service user and their relatives
- ✓ Secure a GP service willing to accept short-term patients from the scheme
- ✓ Acknowledge the physical and social rehabilitation benefits of Intermediate Care
- ✓ Be prepared for initial slow take-up.

❑ 4.7 Extra Care

Chapter 1 outlines the amount of money central Government is spending on Extra Care provision and defines the basic services and amenities offered. This section summarises key principles and issues regarding Extra Care. Readers are strongly advised to browse the relevant Department of Health website and the Change Agent website and Housing Learning and Improvement Network (LIN) referred to in Appendix 1. Much of what follows is taken from the factsheets and other documents on that website, and is used here with the authors' permission.

Extra Care sheltered housing is increasingly popular. There is widespread interest in Extra Care because it:

- Can replace some residential care
- Provides a venue for respite, intermediate and rehabilitative care
- May provide a resource for day centre and other community-based activities
- Reduces pressures on acute services, for example by tackling delayed discharges from hospital
- Is a popular choice amongst many older people.

It is a *concept* rather than a housing type and covers a range of specialist housing models. It incorporates particular design features and has key guiding principles. Extra Care housing can be owned, rented, leasehold, or part owned and part rented. Some developments mix types of tenures. Most Extra Care in the UK is developed with public subsidy by housing associations, but a small private sector exists too.

McCarthy & Stone

McCarthy & Stone established its Assisted Living Division in 1999 to provide much-needed specialised housing for the increasing numbers of frail older people in the private sector. By 2011 owner occupation levels in UK pensioner households is predicted to increase to around 79%.

Assisted Living offers older people a new choice in private retirement housing, which enables them in most cases to retain independence and home ownership for the whole of their lives. There are five key features that distinguish Assisted Living from more traditional private sheltered housing schemes:

- Enhanced design so that the entire scheme is wheelchair accessible
- 24 hour on-site staffing provided by the estate management company
- A waitress service restaurant with on-site catering provides lunches daily at modest cost. Further catering arrangements are available to order
- One hour of domestic assistance is provided each week to every apartment
- Additional domestic and personal care services available to residents upon request by separate arrangements with the domiciliary care agency appointed at the scheme.

To date McCarthy & Stone Assisted Living has completed six schemes comprising a total of 354 units in a mix of one- and two- bedroom apartments and associated communal facilities.

→

A typical scheme would have 50 to 70 apartments, predominantly one-bedroom (75%), with the range of communal facilities within the scheme including a residents' lounge, restaurant, function room, communal laundry, refuse collection room, battery car store, furnished guest suite, communal disabled WCs and lifts to all floors. Staff facilities comprise an Estate Manger's office, a staff suite of dayroom and en-suite bedroom for the overnight sleep-over staff arrangements and a full catering kitchen with associated staff facilities to service the restaurant.

The Company has round 1,000 Assisted Living units in the pipeline from sites exchanged through to sites under construction. Six new schemes are scheduled to open over the next 18 months.

It is important to recognise that Extra Care housing is housing first, and providers should aim to avoid any institutional look or feel to the accommodation. People who live there have their own homes, and legal rights to occupy. This means there is a clear distinction between Extra Care housing and residential care as recognised by the Commission for Social Care Inspection.

The new Housing Corporation definitions for older people's housing no longer use the term "extra care". Instead there is a category "Housing for older people (all special design features)" which stipulates that it is remodelled or purpose-built grouped housing that has all the basic facilities and all special design features intended to enable people to live there for their lifetimes. All the following requirements have to be met:

- **Basic facilities:** the scheme or main building must have basic facilities of a laundry for residents and/or washing machines in living units or provision for washing machines to be installed. The scheme must also have a communal lounge.
- **Special design features:**
  - The whole scheme including entrances and the buildings that comprise it must be designed to wheelchair use standards
  - Living units must have walk-in showers or bathrooms adapted for people with mobility problems or wheelchair users
  - Bathrooms in living units that are wheelchair standard must meet the criteria for adapted bathrooms
  - Living units must have kitchens that are designed to wheelchair standards
  - The scheme must have a bathroom with provision for assisted bathing
  - If there is more than one storey there must be a lift.

Key features of Extra Care housing

Principles

- Focus on individuals
- Rehabilitation
- Independence
- Residents have control – tenancy rights separate from care
- Neighbourliness
- Access to community activities
- Community resource

Design

- Individual flats/bungalows seen as "home"
- Design allows for a range of social activities
- Progressive privacy is built in for residents

Care and leisure

- Flexible care
- Working with, not doing for residents
- 24 hour support
- Care team based in a scheme
- Access to meals
- Domestic support
- Supporting social and leisure opportunities

Assessment and allocation

- Joint assessment and allocation
- Balance of dependency levels
- Positive approach to mental health
- Step up and step down places
- Home for life

Adapted from Fletcher P and Riseborough M et al (1999) *Citizenship and Services in Older Age: The Strategic Role of Very Sheltered Housing*

Good practice checklist: Developing Extra Care in partnership

- ✓ New schemes must be developed only as part of a wider older people's strategy in the locality
- ✓ Planning, commissioning and funding Extra Care has to be done as a partnership between PCTs, social services, housing, Supporting People and regeneration – ideally through a joint commissioning process/board
- ✓ Understand the market – beware of assuming that need comes only from the rented sector
- ✓ There must be a common vision of what commissioners are hoping to achieve and providers expecting to provide
- ✓ A well-networked champion for the proposal is needed in the commissioning structure
- ✓ Create and seize all opportunities to develop trust, clarity and transparency between partner agencies
- ✓ Consider remodelling an existing sheltered scheme – new-build may not be necessary
- ✓ Develop and stick to a clear project plan
- ✓ Define roles and responsibilities of staff from each agency
- ✓ Ensure building design includes: self-contained units (but not bedsits), wheelchair accessible throughout, assisted bathrooms, lifts
- ✓ Ensure service design includes: personal care, 24-hour cover, alarm service, provision of meals, access to preventative health care
- ✓ Ensure social design includes: mix of dependency needs; meeting of social, educational and entertainment needs; lifelong learning opportunities; community participation, access to facilities by non-residents (especially relatives and volunteers)
- ✓ Ensure management includes: active involvement with residents in service design, staff development
- ✓ Explore the wide range of models and structures for Extra Care before selecting 'best fit' for local needs
- ✓ Beware of Extra Care schemes recreating residential care in another name
- ✓ Don't 'reinvent the wheel' – use the guidance and good practice examples on the Change Agent website: www.changeagentteam.org.uk/housing

The Department of Health has published two useful documents to improve the understanding of Extra Care Housing and how to support bidding guidance for its Extra Care Housing grant programme to 2008. These are *Extra Care Housing for Older People: an introduction for commissioners* (2004) and *Developing and Implementing Local Extra Care Housing Strategies* (2004). Both are available at www.changeagentteam.org.uk/housing.

❑ 4.8 Housing for Older People Alliance – HOPA

Currently six national organisations (EAC, ASAP, ARHM, CSHS, ERoSH, AIMS) whose key purposes include promoting, regulating and/or advising on sheltered and retirement housing meet regularly with a commitment to work together to promote sheltered and retirement housing and to share information and good practice. Sometimes all six organisations work together and at other times two or three members may combine to produce joint material. HOPA produced a joint leaflet *Supporting Older People in Making Quality Choices* in 2004. Its intended audience is primarily non-housing professionals, such as advice centre workers, solicitors and accountants advising older people and their families. Sheltered housing staff are encouraged to obtain the leaflet from any of the six participating organisations and distribute them personally to these and other non-housing professionals.

During 2005 all members of HOPA worked with the NHF, CIH, Counsel and Care and the Federation of Black Housing Organisations on the *20/20 Project – a vision for older people's services*. A consultation paper was issued to obtain the views of older people, housing providers, commissioning bodies, MP and others, in parallel with market research.

Recommendations based on the outcome of this consultation and research will be published in autumn 2005. The recommendations from the consultation will then be taken to government and worked towards by HOPA members. The issues covered by the consultation paper include:

- What housing older people will want
- Support services
- Cultural issues
- The market place
- Telecare
- Design standards
- Extra Care housing
- Skills, knowledge and training.

❑ 4.9 Joint working – some examples of the range of local projects

There is much inspiring yet undervalued partnership working between sheltered housing providers, tenants, their families and local non-statutory agencies and communities as the following examples demonstrate.

Helping residents access computers

Rother Homes

While the introduction of computers and related training into sheltered housing is often only associated with staff, some organisations have seen the benefits of also helping residents to access computers.

In an innovative pilot project, residents at two Rother Homes sheltered housing schemes in Bexhill have become enthusiastic computer users and online communicators.

Rother Homes (part of the Horizon Housing Group) and People for Action worked with Hairnet, a national computer and internet training organisation that specialises in working with older people. Hairnet's 'Digital Unite' programmes provide quality training and support for sheltered housing residents anywhere in the UK. Commitment by Rother Homes staff at scheme and senior level was essential to ensure the project's sustainability; for example, managers and head office staff took part in website discussion boards to address residents' issues large and small.

At the end of eleven weeks' training, successful outcomes included:

- Tenants using the internet and emailing friends, family and each other, therefore reducing isolation
- The formation of a computer club – a new focus for shared activity within the scheme
- Tenants sharing time with their grandchildren at the computers
- A great sense of achievement for tenants who had acquired new skills
- Improved communication between residents and the landlord, and between residents at different Rother Homes sheltered schemes.

The pilot is part of Horizon Housing Group's IT for Older Learners commitment.

Waterloo Housing Association

Waterloo Housing Association worked with Age Concern Birmingham, Birmingham Airport and Sutton Muncipal Charities to install eight computers in sheltered housing schemes for residents' use, and provide related training. Training for residents was initially funded through a grant from Birmingham City Council's Lifelong Learning department, and Waterloo has now arranged for A-level pupils from local schools to teach IT skills to residents.

Tackling security problems and anti-social behaviour

In response to problems relating to security and anti-social behaviour, some sheltered housing providers have written specific policies, procedures and guidance on anti-social behaviour. To achieve maximum benefit, providers should work jointly with relevant local and national statutory and voluntary organisations to develop specialised material and training for staff.

English Churches Housing Group

In a local initiative English Churches was an associated partner involved in tackling a range of anti-social behaviour problems affecting a sheltered scheme – such as dog fouling, drunken brawls, illegal and immoral acts, theft, dangerous driving and noise nuisance – through partnership working. The group involved the local police, the police licensing officer, council officials, local councillors, the local church minister and local tradespeople.

As a result of the partnership noisy neighbours were evicted, more police presence during 'after hours drinking' has reduced the drunken brawls and councillors are now reacting more positively to complaints. With the co-operation and funding from the police, community partnership and local charitable trust and English Churches, a CCTV camera was installed on the corner of the scheme to see up and down the road and into the close between the two blocks of the scheme, and a local tradesman has also installed a further camera in support. Tenants at the scheme gave generously towards the installation of the camera.

The council has agreed to sell the misused land to a local tradesman who has given promise of clearance and good use. Local residents, including the sheltered housing tenants are now more confident about reporting anti-social incidents, and community spirit and awareness of each others' concerns has improved.

Intergenerational work

Family Housing Association (Manchester)

Family Housing arranges for tenants from a sheltered scheme to go into local schools to help young children read or to share their skills with the children. One tenant helps despite experiencing short-term memory loss, and the children respond well to her which has improved her confidence.

Hanover (Scotland) Housing Association

When Hanover (Scotland) celebrates the completion of a new sheltered development, the association uses the opening ceremony as an opportunity to create links with local schools and invite the children to participate in the event. Examples of joint initiatives with local schools include:

- Sheltered housing residents helping re-introduce traditional playground games
- Discussion of wartime memories to bring alive history lessons
- Helping children learn traditional skills of baking, cooking and knitting
- Painting competition to encourage children to think about ways in which people of all ages can be good neighbours to each other.

Orbit Housing Association

A piece of ground between an Extra Care scheme and the local first school provided an opportunity for community working and development. Tenants of the scheme wanted a 'secret garden' which would provide the space for quiet contemplation, as well as being environmentally friendly. A discussion with the school established that the project could provide a number of opportunities within the National Curriculum framework.

The children talked to tenants about what they would like to see and then produced a number of designs. The final design incorporates areas of seating, access for those with impaired mobility as well as trees, flowerbeds and areas for wildlife. Having agreed the design the children, parents and tenants' families dug over the ground and began preparing the site for development. During National Tree Week in 2003 the local council provided trees and the local press attended a tree-planting event. Later a local bank agreed to adopt the project for team building events.

On completion the children will be able to use the garden for nature study and some basic conservation work for their curriculum targets. The tenants will have their area for quiet contemplation, and the bank will have an ongoing record of their successful team building. The community will also have a resource of which all can be proud, and several generations have benefited from working together.

Use of sheltered housing facilities by local agencies

London Borough of Greenwich

A range of collaborative projects between the sheltered housing service and local agencies have been set up, including:

- The use of a sheltered flat as an office base for a project for African elders
- Staff training on visual impairment delivered by the RNIB
- The use of communal facilities to provide venues for regular meetings of patients of the Oxleas NHS Mental Health Trust.

Collaboration between disability services and sheltered teams

Rhondda Cynon Taff County Borough Council

The council has established successful partnership working between the disabilities services team and the sheltered housing service. Projects include:

- Social inclusion – service users from the disability team interact with sheltered housing tenants at weekly social activities
- Environmental improvements – service users from the disability team work on environmental improvements to sheltered housing grounds
- Shopping – disability team service users provide shopping assistance for tenants unable to shop for themselves
- Decorating – disability team service users offer a decorating service.

Dance

Central and Cecil Housing Trust

In 2004, in collaboration with the Royal Festival Hall, Central and Cecil ran a dance project at Philip house, a sheltered scheme in Camden. Robert Hylton, a professional dancer and choreographer came to the scheme with a musician and film maker and led a series of dance sessions, combining ballroom dancing steps, reminiscence and modern street dancing. Staff and tenants from the scheme also went to the Royal Festival Hall and took part in two days of filming and the results of the project were incorporated into a short film called 'Two Sugars with my Hip-Hop Please'. This was screened at a public performance by Robert Hylton. All the participants attended and received a standing ovation.

Information resource for older people

Thanet Island Guide

The Island Guide is an information resource in the form of a booklet and website, and was developed through partnership working by Thanet District Council, Thanet Community Housing Association, Kent County Council Social Services, Thanet PCT and Older People of Thanet.

The project was developed after research carried out by Housing 21 identified that older people in Thanet required better quality information, advice and advocacy.

The object of the guide is to provide information on services for older people from a single access point. Statutory organisations worked with older people, many living in sheltered housing, through workshops, presentations and surveys. The involvement of the older community in planning the guide resulted in a wide range of services being covered, including medical, care advice, housing options and social activities.

The guide has attracted much interest and is used by the recently established Pension Service to assist their officers when out on visits. The guide has been recognised as an example of good practice by the Department of Health and the South East Regional Housing Statement. When first issued, demand for the guide far outstripped supply and a second, updated edition was launched in August 2004. The project fully embraces equality and diversity, both in the content and through its dissemination (it can be provided in other languages and formats). Feedback via a users' evaluation questionnaire, the website itself and from other agencies in the voluntary and private sector has been very positive.

The Island Guide can be accessed at www.theislandguide.org

Support Services

Liverpool Housing Trust

The Trust works in partnership with the Merseyside Chinese Community Development Association – Chinese Carers Network to provide a sheltered support service to tenants. The service is aimed at older Chinese tenants, although tenants of other backgrounds who need the service are not excluded.

→

The service offers two hours help per week with tasks such as:

- Help around the home, eg housework
- Minor works, eg changing a light bulb or plug
- Shopping assistance
- Going to the Post Office
- Help with understanding/completing forms and letters
- Chatting, social interaction, arranging social events etc.

The Chinese Carers Network receives Supporting People Grant directly to provide the service. Tenant Support Plans are completed jointly with the Scheme Manager and Support Worker from the Chinese Carers Network. There is a service level agreement in place between LHT and the Chinese Carers Network, and currently 44 tenants benefit from the service.

❑ 4.10 Conclusions

This chapter has demonstrated the:

- Reasons for partnership working at strategic, operational and practice levels
- Benefits of partnership working for service users and organisations
- Plethora of mechanisms, tools and incentives for partnership working
- Range of positive outcomes that it is possible to achieve through partnership working.

CHAPTER 5

QUALITY, STANDARDS AND PERFORMANCE

This chapter describes the range of compulsory and optional reviews, standards, performance indicators, codes of practice and appraisal methods now governing sheltered housing. In particular it outlines:

- Supporting People:
  - background, aims and benefits of the programme
  - key elements of the programme, including the assessment measures used
- Audit Commission inspections of:
  - the delivery and development of the Supporting People programme by Administering Authorities
  - sheltered housing services provided by local authorities and housing associations
- Codes of practice relating to sheltered and retirement housing
- Appraisal toolkits and benchmarking systems relating to sheltered housing

The chapter looks at some challenges faced by sheltered housing providers in meeting these standards, along with examples of benefits and positive outcomes of focusing on performance improvement. Most of this chapter does not apply to retirement housing, with the exception of the Code of Practice of the ARHM (page 114).

Successive governments have required the public sector as a whole to demonstrate:

- A stronger focus on customers
- Value for money
- Greater accountability
- Increased choice
- The achievement of higher standards and better performance
- Self assessment and continuous improvement
- Efficiency.

To achieve these aims a complex structure of regulatory bodies, standards and performance targets and measures govern the statutory and voluntary organisations that provide health and social care, education and housing. In all these sectors there is a recognised emphasis on driving forward service improvements for the benefit of the customer, and sheltered housing has become part of this detailed regulation and contract culture for the first time. For those working in sheltered housing, the Supporting People programme is the main framework for performance improvement.

❑ 5.1 Supporting People

■ Background, aims and benefits for sheltered housing

Introduced in April 2003, Supporting People gave local authorities new responsibilities to plan, fund, commission and monitor housing related support services for vulnerable people, including those provided in rented sheltered housing (see page 15 for explanation of the impact of Supporting People on private retirement housing).

The aims of the programme are to:

- Increase the quality of services for vulnerable people
- Contribute to service users' empowerment and independence
- Support people to make informed choices
- Encourage providers to respond to diverse needs
- Ensure services are cost effective and meet identified needs.

To achieve these aims Supporting People has introduced new systems and requirements which all staff need to understand. For the first time, there are now national, compulsory standards requiring staff at all levels to demonstrate that they are:

- Delivering quality services
- Working towards further improvement
- Working within wider strategic frameworks.

A major rethink of the sheltered housing service was inevitable following the publication in 1998 of *Home Alone*, the Audit Commission's report on housing and community care. In the report, the following criticisms were made of the sheltered housing service:

- Lack of strategy
- Lack of vision
- Tension between lettings and frail older people's needs
- Need for more focused role of warden
- Need for more effective joint working

- Unprotected vulnerable/frail older people
- Lack of service evaluation/target setting/measuring of performance
- Unasked questions of demand and allocation criteria
- Need for maximisation of sheltered housing facilities
- Lack of statutory regulation and inspection re standards and performance.

These and other themes have been incorporated into the Supporting People programme and there is now no escape for providers who continue with the old ways of working.

This new regime has had a huge impact on many sheltered housing providers which have had to adapt to a challenging and totally new contract culture and related scrutiny which establishes whether services merit funding. Under the old system, housing benefit paid for support charges, was uncapped and required no evidence of quality and performance. The ODPM recognises that the challenge for some sheltered housing providers has been very hard – see pages 106-108 (ODPM guidance). However, many providers have seen considerable benefits arising from Supporting People, directly or indirectly, as indicated below.

Cottsway Housing Association

The following benefits were identified from the service review process:

- Improved team work
- Secondment opportunities for scheme staff
- Staff development – project working/training
- Improved communication between staff and tenants
- Increased profile of sheltered tenants and supporting staff within the organisation
- Increased organisation's profile with external stakeholders and commissioning bodies
- Opportunity to reflect on current practices
- Improved service and a platform developed for continuous improvement.

CDS Housing

CDS chairs the NHF Merseyside Providers' Forum, a group with members drawn from health and Supporting People teams, RSLs and local authorities. The Forum considers local issues relating to Supporting People, services to older people and adaptations. A sub-group is developing local benchmarking across a whole range of sheltered issues such as support costs, staff terms and conditions, policies and procedures and relief cover.

→

The group shares good practice and aims to achieve value for money by identifying cost-effective means of delivering services to older people. For example, the sub-group is currently investigating out-of-hours services to sheltered tenants through a mobile response service, which will be facilitated as a partnership venture involving several RSLs.

Derby Homes

Following the introduction of the Supporting People programme, Derby Homes identified a supply and demand mismatch for sheltered housing, and has created an action plan to address it. The options being considered include:

- Using some low demand sheltered housing to accommodate other vulnerable groups and negotiating a revised contract with the local Supporting People team
- Undertaking an Extra Care feasibility study of selected category 2 schemes with local housing, social services and Primary Care Trust strategy officers
- Joint working with equalities officer to link in with the local BME housing strategy and to agree a cross-referral system with a specialist Asian elders sheltered provider
- Attending local hospital social work team meetings to promote existing disability-friendly/adapted sheltered properties and to find out what types of supported accommodation are actually needed.

Dudley Council

Supporting People provided the impetus for Dudley's sheltered housing team to focus on new ways of working and develop partnerships with other agencies to create a comprehensive range of services for older people. The menu of support options now includes the provision of:

- 24/7 home call emergency alarm service available to the council's sheltered housing tenants and to other vulnerable residents living in wider council accommodation and in the private sector
- Specialist services to increase security
- Floating support to older council tenants who live outside sheltered housing via a patch-based visiting warden service
- Purpose-built accommodation with communal facilities and on-site manager
- Housing with care accommodation with on-site care team.

The Supporting People programme places great emphasis on measurable outcomes, and many sheltered housing providers have struggled to demonstrate these given the long-term nature of the support they provide. Managers are encouraged to set up systems to ensure that, over time, improvements and achievement of goals identified in support plans are recorded, pooled and analysed. Self-assessment questionnaires for service users are another way to track and assess outcomes. The following list demonstrates the range and scope of positive potential outcomes for sheltered housing service users.

Potential outcomes for sheltered housing service users

- Increased sense of wellbeing – clients expressing increased sense of wellbeing from assessment to first support plan review
- Increased social contacts, eg numbers of new social contacts made
- Reduced anxiety/depression
- Increased feelings of safety and security
- Correct financial benefits/level of benefit increase
- Appropriate equipment and adaptations
- Health and social care needs met
- Awareness and take-up of culturally appropriate options regarding: housing, social and lifelong learning activities, health promotion activities
- Reduction or prevention of hospital admission
- Number of clients involved in the service, eg numbers attending a client forum
- Improved daily living and self-care skills
- Improved budgeting skills
- Improved personal administration
- Other categories as defined by service users themselves and formally recorded in support plans
- Reduction or prevention of admission into registered care homes
- High rate of take-up of services

Key elements of the Supporting People programme

Chapter 1 (pages 15–17) outlined the broad implications of Supporting People for providers, and the rest of this section sets out the key elements of the programme. Readers are encouraged to refer to the fuller guidance on the Supporting People website at www.spkweb.org.uk. The key elements covered below are:

- Service reviews
- Measures of assessment used in Supporting People, including the Quality Assessment Framework, Core and Supplementary Objectives, and Performance Indicators

- Value for money and cost effectiveness
- Working with the Administering Authority

This section also contains a good practice checklist on preparing for service reviews and working within the contract culture.

Supporting People has introduced new teams:

- **Supporting People Commissioning Body** – commissions support services, including from sheltered housing providers (local authorities and housing associations)
- **Core Strategy Group** – determines strategic direction for support services locally
- **Administering Authority** – manages Supporting People grant contracts and conducts reviews (usually run by the social services department in counties and by either the housing department or by social services in London Boroughs and other unitary authorities).

The Audit Commission's Housing Inspectorate inspects the Administering Authorities to ensure that they are implementing the Supporting People programme in accordance with ODPM requirements and guidance (see pages 108–111 for further information on the framework used and an analysis of some reviews).

Service review

The service review process provides the Administering Authority (AA) with the opportunity to draw together a wide range of information about a service which it has inherited through the creation of the Supporting People programme, including the strategic fit of the service and how it is performing.

The service review is a one-off process, with all services to be reviewed once by April 2006. After that, authorities will be expected to monitor services on an ongoing basis through day-to-day contract management processes.

The main purpose of a service review is to enable Administering Authorities to:

- Determine whether services are meeting the strategic objectives for the Supporting People programme at a local level
- Assess whether there is a continued demand for the service
- Evaluate the quality and performance of services
- Assess the extent to which continuous improvement is taking place
- Risk assess services to inform the future level of monitoring and frequency of validation visits
- Highlight whether significant changes should be considered (eg service remodelling or decommissioning).

The four stages of a service review	
Stage	
Stage 1 **Strategic Review**	**A. Assessment of strategic relevance** *The AA may ask:* • To what extent do the needs being met by the service reflect those prioritised for Supporting People? • To what extent does the type of service reflect those prioritised for Supporting People funds? • How does the service contribute to the Authority's agenda on homelessness/drug and alcohol/crime reduction/health improvement/domestic violence? • How does the service contribute to the Authority's preventative agenda (ie by reducing or delaying the need for more costly services)? • How does the service contribute to the strategic objectives of other stakeholders (eg on hospital discharge)? The Audit Commission has indicated what outcomes are achievable for sheltered housing – see page 93 – and providers are encouraged to work with service users and staff to record outcomes and benefits, prior to the strategic review. **B. Demand for the service** *Sources of information to assess demand for the service* • Information on existing and future needs within the Supporting People strategy based on: – a needs mapping exercise – data on the needs of BME communities – research studies – demographic data – housing and support registers • Supply data – from the SPLS systems • Performance data, such as: – trends in utilisation rates for the service – management data on reasons for service users leaving a service • Other relevant data, such as referrals and waiting list data.
Stage 2 **Desk Top Review of Quality and Performance**	**A. Quality of service** **B. Performance of service** **C. Cost effectiveness** **D. QAF validation visit report (where a validation visit has been undertaken)** →

Stage 2 – contd.	*Validation visits* A typical validation visit to a sheltered housing scheme follows this programme: • Introduction and 'boundaries' setting • Tour of premises, including with a service user • Meeting with staff group • One-to-one meetings with appropriate staff • Lunch • One-to-one meetings with a range of service users • Summary of findings/feedback A validation visit needs to have a clear purpose and function – not ALL service reviews necessarily have a validation visit – depends on the nature of the service and the approach taken locally. *Reasons for involving service users in service reviews* • Users have a right to be involved in decisions that affect them • Authorities should not rely on providers speaking on behalf of their service users • Users are ultimately the best people to describe the quality of the services they receive • A direct line to the authority enables 'whistle blowing' when things are going badly wrong • Users are usually the people who know most about what isn't working for them, and are likely to have good ideas about how to make things better.
Stage 3 Further Evidence/ Service Review Investigation	**A. Further evidence sought** **B. Meetings with provider and stakeholders (if required)** **C. Service review investigation visit (if required)**
Stage 4 Outcome of the Review	***Possible outcomes:*** **A. Renew contract with no changes** **B. Renew contract with changes** **C. Renew contract with action plan** **D. Remodelling of service** **E. Change of provider** **F. Decommission service**

■ Measures of assessment used in Supporting People

The Quality Assessment Framework (QAF)

The Quality Assessment Framework (QAF) has two principal purposes:

- To provide a standardised means for Administering Authorities to assess the quality of services
- To encourage and facilitate the raising of standards in the provision of housing-related support.

It is intended as a tool for providers to work towards continuous improvement and as a structure to carry out their self-assessment and submit it to the Administering Authority (AA).

Providers self-assess their services under six Core Objectives (the compulsory minimum standards) and inform the AA annually of their performance level. During the service review process this self-assessment is tested (validated) and the overall grade contributes to the outcome of the review. This self-assessment can be validated at any time, not necessarily within the service review.

The grades for the Core Objectives and Supplementary Objectives are:

A. Excellent
B. Good practice
C. Minimum standard met but scope for improvement
D. Minimum standard not met – service unacceptable.

Providers must produce for AAs action plans demonstrating how and when they will improve their grades. In order to achieve the higher performance levels (A and B), providers need to have integrated service user involvement into their approach to service management and delivery. Providers assessed at level D grades are prioritised for further investigation by AAs and could lose Supporting People funding if level C is not achieved within the short term.

QAF Lite

Different rules apply to small sheltered housing providers, defined as:

- Those employing no more than one full-time equivalent member of support staff *and*
- Services provided at low weekly SP rates (less than £5 per week at 2004 prices) as part of low value contracts (less than £5000 per year at 2004 prices).

Unlike the main QAF, QAF Lite is not a tool for continuous improvement and the QAF Lite objectives are not assessed against different levels (A to D). Instead level C is used alone, as an indication of compliance. Small providers should read the QAF Lite guidance and Core Service Objective documents on the Supporting People website.

Core Objectives

There are six Core Objectives that set out the minimum requirements for Supporting People. The sub-headings within each standard outline the evidence requirements needed to meet the various performance levels. Providers should use the full ODPM Core Objectives documents available on the Supporting People website (or others provided by their AA) to be sure that they make a comprehensive and honest self-assessment. Many sheltered housing providers find the achievement of level C extremely challenging and are many years from attaining level A, or even B.

Core Objectives – common gaps and potential improvements to services

Core Objectives (CO)		The most frequently missing evidence at reviews*	Improvements in the quality of sheltered housing services as a result of CO
C1.1	**Needs and risk assessment** Assessments of needs and risks are carried out for all service users. Processes place users' views at the centre, are managed by skilled staff and involve carers and/or other professionals.	• Support plan reviews not done • No written procedure • Insufficient connection between pre-tenancy assessment and subsequent support plan • Insufficient training on needs assessment and support planning.	• Needs that were previously overlooked or understated are now identified and steps taken to as address them, eg: – the identification of under-claimed benefits – a more precise assessment of equipment and adaptations needed – loneliness and depression picked up • Lack of understanding of fire procedures, door entry and alarm systems identified and addressed • Staff spend less time on social chat and are more outcome orientated in the use of their time.
C1.2	**Support plans** Service users have up-to-date support plans in place. Processes place users' views at the centre, are managed by skilled staff and involve carers and/or other professionals.		
C1.3	**Security, health and safety** The security, health and safety of all individual service users and staff are protected.	• Risk assessments excluding lone working • No lone working policy • Lack of formal inspections • Insufficient information to residents.	• Increased awareness of lone working risks and consequent steps to minimise them • Greater awareness of range of risks in sheltered housing – related to building, staff, visitors, residents and equipment.

→

C1.4	**Protection from abuse** Service users have the right to be protected from abuse and this right is safeguarded.	• Lack of understanding of abuse policy • Nothing written on proper relationships between staff and tenants • Lack of whistle-blowing policy • No staff criminal records checks.	• Greater awareness of types and indicators of abuse by staff and tenants • Increased knowledge by staff and tenants of what to do, and what not to do, if abuse is suspected.
C1.5	**Fair access, diversity and inclusion** There is a commitment to the values of diversity and inclusion and to practice of equal opportunity (including accessibility in its widest sense) and the needs of black and minority ethnic service users are appropriately met.	• Insufficient information to tenants • Staff induction training insufficient • Lettings/allocations/ equal opportunities policies more than five years old.	• Increased liaison between those responsible for allocations and those responsible for service management • Greater recognition of the range of needs encompassed within the term 'diversity' • More efforts by scheme-based staff and service managers to make links with local BME communities and groups.
C1.6	**Complaints** Users, carers and other stakeholders are made aware of complaints procedures and how to use them.		• Greater attention given to ensuring complaints procedures are fully accessible to, and used by, sheltered housing service users • Complaints monitored and followed as part of the process of continuous improvement.

* Source: I. Parry, research published in *Property People*, April 2004

The introduction of needs and risk assessments and support plans (C1.1 and C1.2) have been particularly challenging for many frontline staff and their managers. Resistance to change has been apparent at all staff levels as well as by tenants. Sometimes the culture in sheltered housing has been reactive rather than proactive, with the scheme manager spending more time than necessary with those who are the most vocal, rather than with quieter residents who may have hidden and unmet needs. Some needs were overlooked in the absence of a system of regular and systematic needs assessment of each tenant. Concerns about the time spent on assessments and support plans can be addressed by evenly spreading reviews over the year.

The following examples show how some organisations have used the Core Objectives to develop good practice.

Nene Housing Society

Nene Housing Society has translated the ERoSH Support Plan into an Access database which enables the collection of relevant data and also the production of simple reports, eg number of people having falls within a set period, dependency levels etc. The database is still being rolled out but is already proving a valuable tool.

Hanover Housing Association

In 2005 Hanover updated its policy, procedures and guidance on the protection of vulnerable adults and has made these available to other providers. The revised version retains the original framework and key information but includes additional:

- Case studies on suspected, alleged and confirmed abuse
- Guidance on dealing with grey areas
- Guidance on the interpretation of definitions of abuse and vulnerable adults
- Guidance on assessment of the situation
- Guidance on risk assessment with a form to assist in this process
- Tips on referral and working with other agencies, in particular with social services
- Tips on preventing and raising awareness of abuse
- Examples of good and poor practice in handling abuse
- Information on Supporting People requirements, including a list of the types of questions that service users and staff could be asked at validation visits as part of service reviews
- Lists of useful national agencies.

The document will help sheltered, retirement and supported housing providers to improve their approach to adult protection. It will also help organisations to meet the quality requirements of the Supporting People programme which requires providers to have robust and up-to-date procedures for preventing and responding to actual or suspected abuse or neglect. See www.hanover.org.uk for more details.

Supplementary Objectives

In addition to the six Core Objectives, there are eleven Supplementary Objectives that are optional and can be agreed by the AA with the provider in the longer term. However the QAF guidance strongly advises providers to take the good practice approach of assessing their services against all seventeen service objectives. The following table shows the standard for each Supplementary Objective and, as for Core Objectives, is the basis for self assessments.

Supplementary Objectives

Group 1 – Empowerment

S1.1 Informing service users: Service users are well informed so that they can communicate their needs and views and make informed choices.

S1.2 Consulting and involving service users: Service users are consulted about the services provided and are offered opportunities to be involved in their running.

S1.3 Empowerment and supporting independence: There is a commitment to empowering service users and supporting their independence.

S1.4 Participation in the wider community: Service users are empowered in their engagement in the wider community and the development of social networks.

Group 2 – Rights and responsibilities

S2.1 Privacy and confidentiality: Individual rights to privacy and confidentiality are respected.

S2.2 Rights and responsibilities: The rights and responsibilities of service users, staff and community are promoted and protected.

Group 3 – The service

S3.1 Service description: The provider has a coherent description of the support service/s to be provided, based on defined values, rights and philosophy of support.

S3.2 Choice, sensitivity and responsiveness: The service is flexible, sensitive and responsive with the aim of maximising service users' dignity, independence, choice and control over their own lives.

S3.3 The living environment: is suitable for its stated purpose, accessible, safe and well maintained; is appropriate to the needs of residents; meets the requirements for independence, privacy and dignity.

Group 4 – Organisation and management

S4.1 Continuous improvement: The service is organised within a culture of continuous improvement. The QAF Framework is used as the basis for ensuring that the key aspects of support service improvement are being described, evaluated and improved.

S4.2 Staff recruitment, management and development: Service quality and improvement are achieved through sound support, management and development of all the people working to deliver support.

Performance Indicators

The Supporting People programme requires support providers to supply the Adminstering Authority (AA) with Performance Indicator (PI) data on a quarterly basis. Electronic workbooks have been supplied to assist providers with this task.

KPIs: There are two Key Performance Indicators (KPIs) relevant to sheltered housing:

1. Maintaining independence
2. Ensuring fair access.

Service PIs: There are four Service Performance Indicators:

1. *Service availability* – the number of units available for letting as a % of the number in the support contract
2. *Utilisation levels* – the number of units occupied as a % of the number of units available
3. *Staffing levels* – the number of hours worked in providing the service as a % of the adjusted establishment support hours
4. *Throughput* – the number of service users using the service during the period as a % of the number of units or support placements contracted. The calculation takes account of the number of service users who have departed as well as those who continue to use the service.

Local PIs: In addition, AAs may determine their own local PIs and providers may also set their own PIs. It is particularly challenging to identify PIs which attempt to measure quality of life. They should reflect local needs and priorities, be set in conjunction with service users and linked to business plans. For further information see www.local-pi-library.gov.uk/index.html

■ Value for money and cost-effectiveness

A key aim of the Supporting People programme is to ensure value for money. This goal became a key driver of the programme following the 'sizing of the pot' to £1.8 billion in 2004, a huge increase on the original tentative estimates of £300,000 in 1999. An independent review in early 2004 stated that this amount of 'legacy funding' was too high and the Government made a commitment to drive costs down. All AAs and service providers must now operate in a climate of cuts until at least 2006 and many providers are consequently struggling to pay salary increases, deal with increased administration and improve support services. Beyond 2006 the future level and nature of funding for Supporting People is unknown and open to speculation.

The Independent Review of the Supporting People programme led to various initiatives to improve value for money. These included the eighteen month Value Improvement Projects (VIP), begun in January 2005, to support the work of local authorities in securing substantial improvements in value for money by improving how authorities contract and manage services. Good practice arising from the work of the VIPs will be collected and disseminated.

Durham County Council

Durham County Council is one of nine VIPS (Value Improvement Projects) and the only project focusing on older people. Durham and Districts Supporting People Partnership is working with providers, partner agencies and commissioners to re-model community alarm and warden services across the county in order to provide more flexible and targeted services with better outcomes for service users. The intended outcome will be the achievement of increased and consistent access to services via a re-contracting process that will feature detailed service specifications with explicit service and pricing structures. The process will feature merging or remodelling of current provision, along with procurement of new provision within agreed cost bandings. The longer term intention is to extend joint commissioning with social care and health and the five primary care trusts to develop a wider range of assistive technologies, telecare and telemedicine services.

Local authorities and housing associations are also working within the government's efficiency agenda, which requires them to achieve efficiency gains in order to achieve better value for money for their tenants. Efficiency is not about cuts in service, but about releasing more resources to fund service improvements and further housing provision. The ODPM has set challenging targets for the housing sector to achieve as a whole.

Good practice checklist: Preparing for Supporting People reviews and meeting ongoing Supporting People contractual requirements

- ✓ Read the relevant guidance on the SP website – www.spkweb.org.uk
- ✓ Designate one person to have overall responsibility for ensuring everyone is prepared for service reviews, but share reading and self assessment tasks across the whole team
- ✓ Use internal auditors to 'reality check' self-assessments
- ✓ Ensure that staff are fully and regularly briefed on Supporting People and that they understand the significance and implications of the new contract culture and the emphasis on outcomes
- ✓ Ensure staff know what to expect if their scheme or service has a validation visit – run training sessions for staff using the ODPM interview scripts for each Core Objective
- ✓ Ensure that tenants understand Supporting People and have been told about the review and know what to expect if review officers come to their scheme and want to talk to them

➔

- ✓ Have a box file of documents and data to match Supporting People requirements at each scheme to be reviewed. Reviewers can take away a full set of up-to-date information; saves trawling for paperwork each time, ensures scheme managers know exactly what is required and is more efficient for the reviewer
- ✓ Prepare detailed action plans (demonstrably involving service users and staff teams) addressing gaps in evidence identified in the self-assessments and demonstrating a commitment to continuous improvement by showing how grades will improve
- ✓ Work in partnership with other local providers to address common issues identified in the local Supporting People strategy such as lack of BME representation, high levels of voids, using scheme facilities for community organisations, insufficient Extra Care provision, professionalisation of staff
- ✓ Produce a short document demonstrating that the service fits the local Supporting People strategy for sheltered housing and delivers tangible outcomes
- ✓ Compare support charges with competitors – unit costs in the top and the bottom quartiles will be more rigorously assessed – focus on driving charges down, not on how costs are made up

■ Working with the Administering Authority

The implementation of the Supporting People programme has been a huge undertaking for all concerned, and there are various ways in which concerns about the process have been addressed by the ODPM, Administering Authorities and service providers. Some concerns expressed in the housing press and elsewhere about the experience of sheltered housing services have included:

- Delivering quality services with reduced funding
- Uncertainty of future funding – speculation regarding allocation formula and non-ring fencing beyond 2007
- Delays in receiving results of service reviews
- Delays in notification of the date of service reviews
- Delayed or insufficient payments, inaccurate schedules, delays in issuing steady state contracts after reviews
- Reviews conducted against level B evidence when only level C self-assessment submitted
- Moving goalposts regarding eligible/ineligible services
- Disproportionate amounts of time taken to provide PI and other data to Administering Authorities and related concerns that this data is not being used by the AA
- Variations between Administering Authorities regarding the interpretation of the ODPM guidance on reviews and the QAF – some AAs adopt a 'light touch' approach, and others are more rigorous

- Difficulties for providers with stock located within several AAs – different requirements despite SP being a central government programme which is now locally owned
- Some reviews done by review officers who have no understanding of the user group
- Perceptions of sheltered housing by some AA staff:
  - difficulty in appreciating the difference between short-term support in most supported housing and the long-term support offered in sheltered housing
  - not appearing to value the changing and preventative nature of support offered
  - difficulty in understanding/accepting that sheltered housing is often let to people moving in with no support needs at the time but who have moved in anticipation of future needs.

To help address some of these concerns the ODPM has:

- Developed and promoted QAF Lite for organisations which qualifiy, and a read-across for the Abbeyfield standard to the main QAF
- Encouraged AAs to 'passport' providers accredited with the CSHS Code of Practice
- Encouraged AAs to cluster their reviews of sheltered housing services, reducing bureaucracy where several schemes are run by the same staff group, using the same policies etc
- Supported joined up approaches by AAs, such as the Greater Manchester example below.

Greater Manchester: Joint approach to reviewing sheltered housing

The ten Greater Manchester Administering Authorities (AAs) have agreed a joint approach to streamline the sheltered housing review processes. This in practice means a consistent approach to the QAF, with an extra column of guidance notes indicating what evidence is acceptable at Level C for the QAF across all ten Administering Authorities. The AAs have also produced a standard template and process for risk and needs assessment and for support planning agreed by all ten authorities.

This initiative is intended to make the review process less arduous for the providers, achieve consistency across the AAs, help AAs progress their sheltered housing reviews and ensure that quality of service and performance improvement is achieved without generating unneccessary bureaucracy. The partnership has now been extended to include Knowsley MBC, and will be offered to all other local authorities in the North West in the future.

Providers have been working to address these issues through dialogue and negotiation with AAs and by:

- Referring to the ODPM guidance on Value for Money, which states that:
  - VFM is a relative concept
  - comparisons are complex – they must be on a reasonably like-for-like basis, recognising that no two services are identical
  - by comparing unit costs of broadly similar services against staff-to-service-user ratios, many services could be reasonably meaningfully compared
  - results of comparisons should be used only to identify those services that have particularly high or particularly low costs – authorities should refrain from focusing on minor differences in costs and should not seek to bring down all costs to those of the lowest regardless of quality BUT authorities should seek to achieve value for the public purse
- Referring to the relevant aspects of the Statutory Guidance (see extract below)
- Referring to the relevant aspects of the section on sheltered housing in the QAF (see extract below)
- Quoting the Service Review, positive practice guide August 2003 which advised AAs *"not to get too bogged down with QAF visits and QAF action plans – the priority for the service reviews is the strategic overview. Detailed work on service quality is also necessary and helpful, but can follow at a more leisurely pace if the overall service is making a positive contribution"*
- Combining with other providers, perhaps through a local ERoSH group, and asking to meet the AA team together
- Drawing on the key areas of success identified in Audit Commission reviews of Supporting People (see page 109).

The following extract from Supporting People Statutory Guidance 31 March 2003 makes clear to Administering Authorities that the sheltered housing service is different in many respects to other supported housing services.

Extract from Supporting People Statutory Guidance 31 March 2003

Sheltered housing plays a preventative role by prolonging independence and self care – for example, by enabling older people to access a range of low level support services that promote their independence and well being. Many tenants enter the sector at a point where they do not yet need support, but wish to be in a tenure where support will be available if and when they require it. Individual tenants' need for support is unlikely to be regular or consistent. Furthermore, sheltered housing may work best where the level of support needed by tenants is varied, providing a good 'mix' of people.

→

> Administering Authorities should show regard to the need to promote choice in sheltered housing, as in other types of housing-related support. ODPM expects Supporting People strategies to recognise this and – as with other client groups – the ability of small or specialist providers to play key roles in the provision of support services should not be prejudiced by purchasing methods.
>
> Authorities must not impose eligibility criteria for entry to sheltered housing that removes choice from older people, removes the opportunity for a balance between those who require lesser and greater levels of support, or dilutes the role of sheltered housing in preventing or delaying the need for people to access acute care.
>
> Where service users have been offered a "home for life" it is essential that residents are able to feel secure in such accommodation.
>
> Administering Authorities should not withdraw funding to support individuals living in services offering a "home for life" on the basis of a Supporting People service review alone. Detailed evidence must be taken into account on all aspects of the scheme – including, but not confined to, the housing-related support it offers. Any decision to withdraw funding should be taken only in the context of a strategic review of sheltered housing in the area.
>
> Whilst ODPM would expect most service agreements and contracts to be subject to robust tendering procedures, there may be certain situations where this will not be appropriate – for example, where the service requires a complex pattern of funding of which the element to be purchased under contract is only one element.
>
> Administering Authorities should consider the extent to which Supporting People services provided by wardens in sheltered housing schemes are inter-linked to those wardens' wider duties when considering the appropriateness of a competitive tendering exercise for such services. Changes of the sheltered service provider will be likely to be exceptional as a result of review.

The QAF guidance April 2004 had a section on the applicability of QAF to sheltered housing. Extracts are quoted below.

> The QAF has been developed as a tool for a wide range of housing related services and as a result may not use language and terms that are tailored to specific service types. This is particularly significant for sheltered housing. When using the QAF to assess sheltered housing services (including almshouses and Abbeyfield services) particular attention should be paid to ensuring that it is used in a way that is appropriate to the service.
>
> →

The assessment of a sheltered housing service user is likely to be much less extensive than that for someone using mental health services for example but should still record the needs of that person as identified when they first move into the service or shortly after or at a subsequent review. It is important to be aware that service users move into sheltered housing as a tenure choice and this may occur before they have a specific or immediate support need. However, these needs are likely to change over time and so it is important to carry out needs reviews and update support plans.

Administering Authorities should recognise the particular demands that the QAF makes on sheltered housing service providers; many of the requirements, in particular the need to formalise assessment and support planning procedures, have been entirely new to sheltered housing. For this reason, in many instances, sheltered housing providers have more work to do to meet the standards set out in the QAF. It is important that Administering Authorities acknowledge this and encourage providers to achieve continuous improvement whilst accepting that the achievement of level C may take a little longer for sheltered housing services.

■ Support services and buildings – separate funding regimes

For RSL sheltered housing providers, a potential future problem arises from the fact that support services (through the Supporting People programme) are now funded and inspected separately from the funding and regulation of buildings (still the responsibility of the Housing Corporation). The new Housing Corporation definitions of housing for older people concentrate on the requirements of the buildings, and there are no specifications or standards for support – the definitions simply state that there must be "access to support".

It is not yet known how Supporting People Administering Authorities will address the implications of the new definitions, but the situation could arise that some AAs may not renew SP contracts for support services delivered in buildings which do not reach the high design standards of "housing for older people (all special design features)" and "housing for older people (some special design features)". This could raise questions about the future use of all those schemes that fall into the third category of "designated supported housing for older people".

❑ 5.2 Audit Commission

The Audit Commission's Housing Inspectorate conducts two types of inspection relevant to sheltered housing:

1. An assessment of the implementation, delivery and development of the Supporting People programme by Administering Authorities
2. Measuring the effectiveness and efficiency of sheltered housing services provided by local authorities and housing associations.

The methodology for both types of inspection includes:

- Self-assessment
- A star rating system to indicate the quality of service (one, two or three stars)
- A grading system of prospects for improvement (poor, uncertain, promising, excellent)
- Key Lines of Enquiry (KLOEs): each KLOE contains sets of questions and statements designed to provide inspectors and others with a framework through which to view and assess services. Descriptions of excellent and fair services are included. There are two specific KLOEs – 10 and 11 – relating to Supporting People and supported and sheltered housing. For further details see the Audit Commission website www.audit-commission.gov.uk/kloe/housingkloe.asp

■ Inspections of the implementation, delivery and development of the Supporting People programme by Administering Authorities

(See details of KLOE 10 – Supporting People – on the Audit Commission website, address above)

The Audit Commission manages inspections of the delivery and development of the Supporting People programme by the 150 Administering Authorities in England. These inspections are likely to have less direct impact on sheltered housing staff than do inspections of individual organisations or reviews by AAs, but providers are encouraged to keep abreast of these published inspection reports as they contain:

- Succinct reminders of the key aims of the Supporting People programme
- Good practice by some AAs in helping providers to achieve these aims
- Useful guidance on the appropriate roles and tasks of the Commissioning Body and the Core Strategy Group.

Where Administering Authorities have been judged to be performing well, some areas of success have included:

- Robust systems in place – for contracting and payments, for service reviews
- Positive relationships with service providers
- Innovative approaches to needs assessments
- Clear analysis of strategic links
- Service reviews
  - clear and shared methodology
  - monitoring and reporting systems in place
  - positive outcomes for service users
- Value for money
  - clarity around eligible services
  - evolving clarity including benchmarking
  - robust analysis
  - identified savings

- Outcomes for service users
  - improved services
  - greater independence
  - new services
  - improved/ new support plans
- Effective partnership working
  - providers
  - health
  - probation.

In some inspections, areas for concern about Administering Authorities' progress have included:

- Governance and delivery:
  - lack of focus and purpose by Commissioning Bodies and Core Strategy Groups
  - corporate commitment and partnerships weak between departments, elected members and officers, frontline and management staff, with no mapping/pooling of knowledge/skills and resources
- Strategic relevance and understanding poor by senior and middle managers and by frontline staff
- Diversity – poor engagement across user groups, exclusions of hard-to-reach and unpopular groups, lack of corporate links
- Engagement with service users weak
- Outcomes for service users not considered in planning and implementation.

■ Inspections of the effectiveness and efficiency of sheltered housing services provided by local authorities and housing associations

(See details of KLOE 11 – Supported Housing – on the Audit Commission website, address above)

KLOE 11 on Supported Housing covers the following areas:

- Access, customer care, user focus including involvement in support plans
- Diversity
- Stock investment and asset management
- Income management, including housing and support charges
- Service user involvement
- Tenancy and estate management
- Allocations and lettings, including support planning
- Value for money.

In its inspection reports, the Audit Commission has highlighted both areas of positive practice and weakness in local authority and RSL sheltered housing. Some examples of these are set out below:

Areas of Positive Practice	Areas of Weaknesses
• High satisfaction among sheltered housing residents • Innovative approaches to consultation and resident involvement • Development of specific sheltered housing tenant compacts • Excellent data management systems for recording resident information including support plans, needs assessments • High level service standards • Committed, customer focused staff • Provision of additional services through partnership working • Comprehensive procedure manuals which promote consistency and high standards • Proactive approach to the publicity and marketing of sheltered housing schemes • Sensitive repairs and maintenance • Efficiency savings achieved through innovative procurement and partnering arrangements.	• Inconsistencies in service delivery • Low levels of awareness or services to meet needs of BME communities • Lack of comprehensive data on dependency levels • Role of scheme manager not defined, leading to problems, risks and inappropriate care burden on staff, and unrealistic expectations by tenants, relatives and care agencies • Contribution of services not evaluated and therefore contribution to independent living overlooked or underestimated • Lack of clarity about costs and charges • No or inadequate performance monitoring • No clear and challenging aims for the service.

❑ 5.3 Codes of Practice relating to sheltered and retirement housing

In common with many other services, sheltered and retirement housing has various Codes of Practice that set and govern standards. There are three principle Codes (CSHS, ARHM, ASAP) covering this sector and providers are encouraged to work towards their adoption, where applicable, in order to maintain and demonstrate good practice.

■ CSHS

The CSHS (formerly the Centre for Sheltered Housing Studies) has administered the Code for over ten years. It is externally assessed and validated and has been endorsed by the ODPM as fulfilling the requirements of the QAF – the Core Service Objectives and the Supplementary Objectives. The diagram below demonstrates the mapping between the two frameworks.

Mapping of CSHS Code of Practice to Core Objectives of April 2004 QAF		
Core Objectives		**Relevant Code Standards which demonstrate compliance with QAF level C**
C1.1	Needs and Risk Assessment	Standards 2 & 8
C1.2	Support Planning	Standards 2, 4, 7 & 8
C1.3	Security, Health & Safety	Standards 9 & 8
C1.4	Protection from Abuse	Standards 9, 5, 6 & 8
C1.5	Fair Access, Diversity & Inclusion	Standards 1 & 8
C1.6	Complaints	Standard 2

Having achieved compliance with the Code, in order to maintain their accreditation providers must demonstrate how their service is working towards levels B and A as part of the process of continuous improvement which is an integral aspect of the Code.

The Code is a set of ten behavioural standards which relate to the provision of a well-organised, good quality sheltered housing service for older people. Compliance with the Code requires organisations to measure and review their services against nationally agreed standards. Compliance is externally assessed by members of an independent panel of sheltered housing consultants, through the inspection of a portfolio of evidence and a visit to the organisation to verify that good practice is implemented throughout the service. The process of working towards the Code enables organisations to update policies and practices, encourages continuous improvement and prepares them for the requirements of Supporting People.

The Code requires organisations to demonstrate that they have clear policies and procedures relating to the following ten standards:

1. Equality of opportunity/diversity
2. Rights and responsibilities
3. Confidentiality
4. Independence and empowerment
5. Service delivery, review and continuous improvement
6. Professional role and responsibilities
7. Collaboration and community development
8. Trained and supported staff
9. Policy and legislation
10. Physical environment

Each of the ten standards sets an objective for policy and practice relating to a key aspect of the sheltered housing service. Compliance with each standard requires the organisation to provide sufficient evidence to demonstrate that they meet the objective. Two different types of evidence must be presented:

1. Policy and strategy evidence (statements, organisational publications etc)
2. Operational evidence of implementation.

The key policy evidence or 'building blocks' include:

- Clear mission for the service, clear aims and objectives
- A procedure manual
- Written information for service users
- Policies on equal opportunities, training, confidentiality, consultation, resident involvement, health and safety, medication, abuse, food hygiene, lone working, lifting and handling, managing hard-to-let properties
- Methods of service review
- Complaints procedures
- Performance indicators
- Appraisal system
- Programme of regular support and supervision
- Commitment to self appraisal of wider logistical, financial and strategic viability of the sheltered housing service, as outlined in the Starfish Appraisal Toolkit (see page 117).

Benefits of working for and achieving the CSHS Code of Practice cited by participating organisations include the following:

- Identified gaps and inconsistencies, therefore enabled these gaps to be addressed (via training and a new procedure manual) and a more consistent service introduced with explicit service standards
- The close link to the Quality Assessment Framework meant that necessary improvements were identified and addressed in advance of the Supporting People review – sufficient evidence was to hand to demonstrate that an effective support service was being provided
- Identified the need to move from a generic management structure to specialist
- Improved partnership work at operational and strategic levels
- Enhanced service user involvement
- Greater 'ownership' and use of policies and procedures – eg implementation of previously underused diversity strategy leading to greater use of voluntary agencies for translation services.

■ Association of Retirement Housing Managers (ARHM)

The first version of the Code, approved by the Government and recognised by the Housing Corporation, was published in 1996 and an addendum added in 1998. A revised Code is expected to be published in 2005. The Code is intended to promote best practice in the management of leasehold residential properties or retirement housing in England and Wales. It is a condition of membership of ARHM that members accept the Code and follow its requirements (subject to restrictions in individual leases). The requirements of the Code are used by Leasehold Valuation Tribunals when addressing management problems in the sector.

The 1996 Code covers good practice and legal requirements regarding:

- Service charges – accounting, budgeting and collection
- Management fees
- Repairs and maintenance
- Services
- Contractors
- Insurance
- Wardens and other staff
- Care services
- Consultation and provision of information
- Residents' associations and recognised tenants' associations
- Complaints procedures
- Resales
- New schemes
- Equal opportunities
- Confidentiality and access to information.

The 2005 Code will include new legal rights arising from the Commonhold and Leasehold Reform Act. The new Code will set higher standards and in particular will require all ARHM members to offer access to an independent redress scheme for disputes.

■ Association of Social Alarm Providers (ASAP)

The Code of Practice was first published in 1998 and has since been expanded and refined. Its purpose is to establish standards for the operation of social alarm and telecare services. The Code provides a robust framework of key outcomes by which a service should be judged. Accreditation against the Code is achieved by independent inspection and lasts for three years with annual interim inspections a requirement of the process. The achievement of the Code of Practice ensures that customers of social alarm and telecare services receive safe, reliable, consistent and continuous provision of high quality customer service. Operational, managerial and technical mechanisms to achieve these outcomes are supported by a series of good practice guides published by the Association.

The process of delivering a social alarm or telecare service splits into three distinct business activities and the Code therefore covers each aspect separately:

- Part 1 – Call handling operations – sets the standards required for the planning, management and operation of social alarms receiving centres – revised version issued in 2002.
- Part 2 – Dispersed alarm operations – sets the standards required for the planning, management and installation of social alarms in the homes of service users, issued in 2002.
- Part 3 – Mobile response operations – sets the standards required for the planning, management and delivery of routine and/or emergency mobile response services, to be issued in 2005.

Members of ASAP have to be independently assessed against the Code of Practice in order to achieve accreditation. Independent assessment establishes that the organisation's documented processes at strategic and operational levels are appropriate and effective in delivering the required outcomes and recognised by ASAP as fully meeting the requirements of the Code. There are currently over 40 service providers which have achieved accreditation to the ASAP Code of Practice Part 1 and more than 10 organisations which have achieved accreditation to Part 2. Many more organisations are working towards achieving these standards as the stature of the Code grows.

The ODPM has cited the Code of Practice Parts 1 and 2 as the applicable standard for those service providers working within the Supporting People Quality Assessment Framework. Work is currently under way to consolidate this position and to achieve 'passporting' status for those organisations that achieve the Code of Practice. In addition Part 3 of the Code of Practice is also referenced within the Supporting People Quality Assessment Framework.

In order to support the status of the Code of Practice within the Supporting People Framework and to reflect the evolving nature of social alarm technology and telecare, the Code of Practice has undergone a full review and will be launched at the end of 2005.

❑ 5.4 Appraisal toolkits, benchmarking and other methods of assessing and improving services

Codes of practice are all-embracing and, usually, externally accredited validations of good practice. In addition, providers may benefit from using some of the self-assessment toolkits that have been designed for the sheltered and retirement housing sector. These toolkits can help providers examine key issues, such as performance improvement and asset management, in a structured and systematic way. Benchmarking is one way that can help providers learn from each other by sharing information and adopting best practice to improve performance.

HouseMark

HouseMark is working with the National Housing Federation and SITRA on a benchmarking project funded by the ODPM around Supporting People provider-led benchmarking. The model is currently being piloted with interested providers, and aims to enable service providers to find practical solutions to dealing with the challenges of benchmarking and:

- Scrutinise costs more effectively
- Identify achievable efficiency gains and critical resource requirements
- Take a more balanced management approach – addressing both costs and quality
- Manage risks associated with externally driven opportunities and changes, eg Supporting People grant allocations, local funding priorities, and procurement processes.

Service providers can also benchmark sheltered housing via HouseMark's housing management benchmarking service. For more details about subscription and consultancy services see the HouseMark website www.housemark.co.uk

Housing Quality Network (HQN)

The HQN offers two specific measures to help sheltered housing providers improve service quality:

- Sheltered housing services workbook to self-assess Best Value
- Benchmarking Club

The sheltered housing services workbook is aimed at helping local authorities and housing associations undertake an honest assessment of their provision and performance in sheltered housing and plan for continuous improvement. The workbook suggests a range of reality checks that should be carried out prior to inspection; it also focuses on the six key questions that the inspectors will ask and the two key judgements that these should inform.

The HQN Sheltered Housing Benchmarking Club seeks to assist members in comparing the provision of their sheltered housing services against a selected peer group. It facilitates this through a questionnaire which, when completed and analysed, gives members the opportunity to meet and discuss the outcomes. For information on joining the HQN see www.hqnetwork.org.uk

■ Starfish

Starfish developed a freely downloadable toolkit, with Housing Corporation funding, to help sheltered housing providers address several agendas at the same time:

- Prepare for Supporting People
- Implement Best Value
- Respond to the changing needs and preferences of older people
- Develop an asset management strategy
- Provide internal quality assurance purposes.

The toolkit breaks down the appraisal process into a number of components: external strategic viability, service quality, physical viability, logistical viability, financial viability, internal strategic viability. There is a questionnaire for gathering feedback from local authorities and other external stakeholders, and the toolkit incorporates the standards from the CSHS Code of Practice.

Hereward Housing

Hereward conducted Starfish appraisals on its sheltered and Extra Care schemes over a six month period from July 2003 to January 2004 as part of a countywide Best Value review. Seven other sheltered housing providers took part. The Starfish model provided a systematic framework within which to assess schemes in a portfolio and thereby set investment priorities. Whilst the exercise did not produce any surprising or unexpected conclusions it provided a structure for bringing together objective and qualitative information to help take what can often be problematic decisions.

Riverside Cheshire

Riverside Cheshire used the Starfish Appraisal Toolkit to carry out a review of its sheltered housing schemes. The toolkit provided a method to appraise individual sheltered schemes in a structured and comprehensive way, so that decisions about their future are based on a sound assessment. The fact the toolkit could be sub-divided into the six principles enabled tasks to be allotted to individual officers with specialist skills and experience. The toolkit informed Riverside about future investment needs and service provision requirements, enabling them to ensure that schemes can meet future demands and are sustainable. The toolkit also reinforced opinions in a structured way rather than an anecdotal way.

Northern Housing Consortium

The Northern Housing Consortium, with Housing Corporation funding, developed a toolkit and methodology by which sheltered housing providers can carry out peer reviews of sheltered housing services. The toolkit provides a detailed summary of the current state of a sheltered housing service and an improvement plan with guidance on how it can be implemented.

The Elderly Accommodation Counsel (EAC)

EAC provides a range of services that can be used by landlords, managers and potential residents to appraise sheltered and retirement housing from a customer perspective.

The **HOOP** (Housing Options for Older People) tool is a self-appraisal tool that helps older people assess in a holistic way both the benefits and disadvantages of moving home compared to staying put. Its strength lies in the way it focuses on and reaffirms the individual's personal preferences and priorities. Several sheltered housing providers have found it a powerful tool to help them understand better what attracts customers to sheltered housing, what specific features they most value, and what information they need to differentiate between sheltered settings. A short form of the HOOP tool ('mini-HOOP') is also available.

EAC's **Housing Options database** aims to describe all UK sheltered and retirement housing schemes in a way that helps potential residents understand clearly what each provides. Planned enhancements will incorporate further detail, and apply a 'lifestyle classification' methodology, already successfully used for residential care homes, to indicate differences in culture and ethos between sheltered schemes and between their landlords or managers.

The website www.housingcare.org is a collaborative venture, initiated and managed by EAC. It provides access to the HOOP tools, Housing Options database and a range of information materials for individuals, housing advisers and providers – including good practice guides and materials.

EAC's free **Advice Line** service delivers impartial information and advice to around 10,000 callers a year, including older people, their families, carers and professionals. Some 70% of enquiries are from or on behalf of older people thinking of moving to sheltered housing. EAC produces an annual analysis of enquiries based on the data it records about each client, and can also provide more specific information and commentary about customer perceptions of sheltered housing, levels of demand by area, tenure preferences and so on. EAC plans to supplement this market intelligence function by working with market research company STRC to recruit a national panel of older people whose views can be tracked on a regular basis.

■ Care and Repair England

A checklist of good practice for providers of social rented housing is included in Care and Repair's evaluation of pilot housing options advice services; see the Housing Options section on the website www.careandrepair-england.org.uk The website offers other information and advice about enabling older people to make an informed choice about moving home versus staying put.

❑ 5.5 Conclusions

This chapter has described and commented on the extensive range of compulsory and optional ways that sheltered housing services can be evaluated and improved. Supporting People is the principal but not the only framework for the improvement of service standards. A wide range of Codes, toolkits, benchmarking and appraisal methods are available for sheltered and retirement housing. Providers are urged to investigate each in more detail, adopting a combination of approaches that will be the most effective for their organisation.

CHAPTER 6

MAKING IT HAPPEN – MANAGING THE SERVICE

The service manager is responsible for ensuring the effective operation of today's sheltered housing service, and preparing for the future. Today's sheltered housing must be led by knowledgeable managers who understand the demands on the service, and can operate at both strategic and operational levels, maintaining and developing partnerships, while ensuring support, supervision and training is in place for scheme-based staff.

This chapter looks at:

- Strategies and structures for the sheltered housing service
- The key role and tasks of the service manager
- Training and support for scheme managers as a dispersed workforce
- Promoting service users' choice and control
- Resolving disputes in sheltered housing.

❑ 6.1 Service strategies and structures

For leadership to be effective, an appropriate service structure must first be in place, together with a clear service strategy, backed up an action plan for delivery. It is the service manager's role to ensure the strategy is implemented, and delivered at operational level by scheme-based staff.

To ensure its survival, the older peoples' housing service provided by each organisation in every local area must be able to respond fully to current and projected local demand, and must provide a quality service to its users. The Supporting People programme, in which sheltered housing plays such an important role, brings all this together. Strong and knowledgeable service leadership is required to meet these challenges.

Leadership of the service calls for:

- A good knowledge of the current quality and inspection regimes, and the tools available to assist with these – covered in Chapter 5
- The ability to maintain and develop strategic partnerships – covered in Chapter 4
- An awareness of the increasing diversity of current and future service users, and of how services can meet a wide range of needs effectively – covered in Chapter 3
- Effective and ongoing support to scheme managers, who are in the front line of delivering Supporting People. The changing role of scheme managers is explored within Chapter 2, while the support and training needed to support the changing role is covered within this chapter.

Service strategies

A clear vision and aims for the service are required, encompassed within an effective service strategy which reflects local need, plans for the present and the future, and demonstrates the organisation's commitment to the delivery of a responsive service to clients by a professional and well-trained workforce.

The service vision, strategy and aims provide the framework for devising an action plan for service delivery.

Nene Housing Society

Nene Housing Society has based its sheltered housing service vision and aims on the government's *"integrated, holistic, inclusive, involving and preventative"* approach to housing and service provision for older people. Nene's sheltered housing service offers:

- Homes of choice to older people
- Support tailored to individual needs, which can change over time
- A home for life subject to the availability of appropriate care and support which can be accessed through the scheme manager, as enabler
- A home environment which residents see as safe and secure
- Promotion of independent living which delays/avoids the need for residential care
- An environment offering varied, positive opportunities for social interaction and stimulation
- Tenancy rights and involvement in decision-making.

Twin Valley Homes

Twin Valley has produced a five-point action plan arising from its sheltered housing strategy:

- Partnership working with social services, primary care trust and voluntary organisations
- Consultation and participation with current and potential residents and lifeline clients
- Marketing the sheltered housing and community alarm services
- Review of service provision and the administrative systems in place
- Consideration of the long-term future and viability of the sheltered housing stock.

Service structures

A strategy for sheltered housing can only be delivered if the service is structured appropriately. To meet current demands more effectively, many organisations have reviewed and re-structured their services, to better facilitate a more cohesive approach, and ultimately, to improve delivery at the front line, as the following approaches show.

South Somerset Homes

South Somerset recognised that its generic area office structure, where staff had been responsible for both general needs and sheltered housing operational matters, was not an effective way of meeting the increasing complexities and demands that came with the Supporting People regime. Instead it combined both the strategic and operational functions and created a team of specialist staff running all aspects of both sheltered and supported housing.

This has assisted greatly with undertaking a review of the overall service and in creating more consistency across the 53 sheltered schemes. There is now more focus on Supporting People objectives and at the same time an improvement to the individual support offered to the scheme managers.

Some organisations have set up separate departments or subsidiary organisations, sometimes with different names as in the following examples, in order to separate the landlord function from the more specialist support and contract management functions.

Metropolitan Housing Trust and StepForward

Metropolitan Housing Trust (MHT) radically revised its structure in response to the Supporting People regime by splitting the landlord and support functions. The MHT regions, managed through housing management teams, retained the landlord functions. MHT established StepForward, a corporate department, to manage the support function responsible for all Supporting People contract management.

Sheltered housing is now managed through a specialist housing function with housing officers who deal with older people, and a housing manager who is responsible for overseeing the landlord function, while the sheltered scheme managers are managed within StepForward. Clear working protocols have been established to ensure that responsibilities for all aspects of the landlord service are clearly set out.

Circle 33 and EPIC Trust

In response to the demands of different workloads the Circle 33 Group has separated housing management from support, to enable clearer specialist functions and a better recognition of the contract culture within which sheltered housing now operates.

The resulting specialist organisation, EPIC Trust, delivers supported and sheltered housing in a contract management mode, focusing on operational matters and on strategic relationships with funders. Epic Trust's Elders Division can focus service delivery towards locally preferred models across the boroughs where they work. Service delivery is based on clear quality mechanisms, including the CSHS Code of Practice, and on QAF planning.

Good practice checklist: Effective sheltered housing service structures

- ✓ The structure must provide for knowledgeable specialists to manage the service.
- ✓ Service managers must operate at a strategic level within the structure.
- ✓ The structure must reflect the need for the sheltered housing service to operate within a contract culture and to develop strategic partnerships.
- ✓ The structure must facilitate support to scheme-based staff with the delivery of quality services at scheme level.

❑ 6.2 Putting the strategy into practice

Despite the positive changes many organisations have achieved by reviewing service structures and transforming the 'warden' role into that of properly-managed scheme manager (as set out in Chapter 2), there is evidence that service managers still face serious challenges. Feedback from Supporting People Administering Authority teams who undertook some of the earliest reviews of sheltered housing, combined with the outcomes of some of the Audit Commission inspections of the delivery and development of the Supporting People Programme raise some areas of concern – see pages 98-99 and page 109.

Criticisms of some organisations include:

- Lack of knowledge of Supporting People requirements, including grant conditions, in respect of support planning by scheme-based staff
- Lack of communication between management and scheme-based staff
- Lack of appropriate management of scheme-based staff
- Lack of shared understanding and engagement with key partners – health and social care providers
- Poor understanding of the strategic relevance of sheltered housing to meeting the needs of older people by senior and middle managers as well as frontline staff
- Little or no older peoples' participation in designing and reviewing services
- Local sheltered housing services not set up, or insufficiently sensitive, to meet the needs of the wider community of older people, such as BME older people.

Such deficiencies can only be addressed within a culture of effective service leadership, and in particular where:

- The line manager possesses relevant expertise and an understanding of the range of strategic issues which impact on sheltered housing and older people today
- There are clear lines of communication between the service manager and frontline staff
- Scheme-based staff are managed within a structure and system which allows for regular supervision and support
- Partnership working actively fosters a shared understanding of the needs and aspirations of older people and the contribution of appropriate sheltered and retirement housing in meeting these.

■ A framework for leading and developing the service

The ERoSH Checklist for Sheltered and Retirement Housing Providers is a valuable tool which not only provides a framework for leading and developing the service, but also illustrates the wide range of knowledge and skills now required of the service manager.

The aim of the checklist, revised and re-issued in 2004, is to provide an *aide memoire* for service managers, summarising the tasks that they must accomplish to ensure the staff, the schemes and the service are ready for the challenging environment in which they now operate. The newly revised version encompasses some of the new activities which Supporting People requires, in particular:

- Brief and train staff for their new roles within Supporting People
- Consider the 'strategic fit' of sheltered schemes within the local Supporting People strategy
- Discuss the community use of sheltered and retirement housing facilities with residents and with strategic partners
- Implement the assessment of care and support needs as part of the allocation process, or at least before the resident moves in
- Ensure that needs and risk assessment and support plans are in place, and that staff are trained to use them effectively.

The checklist asks 32 questions about the strategic and operational aspects of running the sheltered and retirement housing service. An extract is shown below, and the full version is available free of charge via the ERoSH contact details given in Appendix 1.

Extract from ERoSH Checklist for Sheltered and Retirement Housing Providers

Assessment and procedures

		Yes	No	In progress
12	Do you arrange for care and support needs to be assessed as part of the allocation process, or at least before the resident moves in?	❑	❑	❑
13	Do application forms record care and support needs as well as housing needs?	❑	❑	❑
14	Are needs assessment and support plans in place and staff trained to use them effectively?	❑	❑	❑
15	Do you regularly assess levels of dependency in schemes and the impact on service delivery on each site?	❑	❑	❑

→

	Yes	No	In progress
16 Are sheltered and retirement housing staff involved in the allocation process – if not, could they be?	❑	❑	❑
17 Do staff have an up-to-date manual of procedures for assessment of care and support needs, hospital discharge, medication and the help they can give in an emergency?	❑	❑	❑
18 Does the community care/single assessment form adequately deal with housing need, eg whether sheltered and retirement housing would reduce or help to meet a person's care and support needs?	❑	❑	❑

The ERoSH checklist reflects the balancing act between strategic and operational tasks which is a key aspect of the service manager's role. To quote the Head of Community Services at South Somerset Homes:

> *"Supporting People has resulted in a clear need to bring operational and strategic planning together so there is less opportunity for mixed messages or competing priorities. The combining of operational and strategic management has led to a more focused approach to everything we do."*

Partnership activities, examined in detail in Chapter 4, are crucial to the long-term development of the service, and the service manager must take the lead in ensuring these partnerships are fostered and developed.

South Somerset Homes

The introduction of Supporting People has meant that organisations can no longer plan their services and strategies in isolation. This has led to a significant increase in networking groups across Somerset involving the Supporting People teams and other service providers. As a large provider of sheltered housing, South Somerset has been a key participant at these groups, and has found that most forums provide an excellent two-way exchange of information, and give an opportunity for each provider to feed back on how they are responding to the new environment.

South Somerset Homes has also worked closely with social services, the Supporting People team and care providers in setting up a new county-wide contract and specification for Extra Care housing.

Central and Cecil Housing Trust

Central and Cecil works closely with the Supporting People teams and with each partner local authority. Representatives attend all local Supporting People Forums, have liaised with the Supporting People teams to develop effective working relationships and have invited Supporting People managers to speak at the annual residents' conference and staff development days.

Reviewing the sheltered housing service to ensure it matches with the local Supporting People strategy and that it is in a position to meet current and future demand is a key element within all current service strategies.

Twin Valley Homes

Twin Valley Homes involved eight members of staff and two resident volunteers in carrying out a sheltered housing review over a period of six months. The resulting service improvement plan will lead to:

- A rationalisation of the sheltered housing units in terms of staff hours worked at each scheme
- Faster reletting, so reducing void rental loss
- A rationalisation of hard-to-let schemes
- An improvement in the condition of existing stock so making property more attractive to let
- The development of new sheltered housing stock ensuring long-term viability of the service.

The service manager is responsible for leading scheme reviews, but the process must fully involve the scheme manager. In order to assess the continued viability of each scheme, a review should include its physical condition, void levels, value for money, strategic relevance in the local and national context, staffing, and social and community activities.

Accord Housing Association

Each of Accord HA's sheltered housing schemes has its own business plan which is updated each year. The business planning process offers an opportunity for the scheme manager to step back from the day-to-day management of the scheme, and participate with the service manager in reviewing the scheme's current position and future potential.

→

The following issues are included:

- A brief statement of the aims and objectives of each scheme
- Description of the scheme including the number and size of the accommodation, communal spaces and support services
- Demand for the scheme
- Privacy and dignity issues such as shared accommodation
- Compliance with Disability Discrimination Act 1995
- Accessibility for clients with specific needs such as physical, visual and auditory requirements
- Staffing
- Health and safety
- Tenant participation
- Finance issues relating to the scheme including charges and income
- Risk
- Performance
- Three year plan.

Scheme business plans are reviewed individually at scheme manager's one-to-one meetings, and business plan discussion is also a standard agenda item at the quarterly sheltered scheme managers' meetings. The whole process helps to develop the future of the service, feeding into the overall strategy for sheltered housing as well as into Accord's corporate business plan.

Supporting People guidance encourages providers to consider the 'strategic fit' of their provision within the wider local framework of provision for older people. However, some Supporting People authorities have not yet developed their older people's strategies, and this can be frustrating for providers who are planning ahead, as noted by the service manager at StepForward, whose provision crosses the boundaries of several Supporting People authorities:

> *"The strategic 'fit' of our service is yet to be tested, as local strategies are only just emerging. We have always reviewed our existing schemes to ensure they are fit for purpose. Now though we need to await the outcome of the '5 Year Strategies' to see where our schemes 'fit'. We now attend the various SP Forums, but it is evident that there is a wide variation within the different SP Authorities in relation to their understanding of, and capacity to develop SP Older Persons Strategies. Developing new services appears to be very confused at the minute. There do not appear to be clear commissioning strategies."*

Service Manager, StepForward (March 2005)

The emphasis that Supporting People places on strategies and responses which meet local needs leads to a new challenge for service managers who work within organisations with sheltered provision across a range of Supporting People authorities. Not only must the service manager ensure that regular liaison with all the relevant Supporting People authorities takes place, fostering and maintaining the partnerships which are so crucial to the future of the sheltered schemes which they manage, they must also remain fully aware of the varying emphasis and approach to older people's provision which may be in place within each of these authorities. This can be particularly time-consuming where managers have responsibility for a large geographical spread of schemes, exacerbated when the organisation has only a few schemes within a particular Supporting People authority area.

❑ 6.3 Training and support for scheme managers

Sheltered and retirement scheme managers have always been members of a dispersed workforce. Located away from their organisation's headquarters where policies, procedures and key decisions are produced, dispersed workforce members have relatively little contact with their line manager and other colleagues.

Given the greatly changed environment in which sheltered housing now operates, service managers have a key responsibility to ensure that, while scheme managers may still be physically some distance from headquarters, they have regular opportunities for training, support and information exchange.

Calico Housing

Calico has recognised that staff working away from the main office can feel isolated, underestimated and undervalued. The organisation is currently undergoing a service review and will evaluate staff roles, taking into account how a dispersed team operates. Calico has also acknowledged that the team is an untapped resource for the organisation, and is looking to provide opportunities for the dispersed staff to contribute their knowledge and experience and to raise their profile within the organisation.

Supporting People has both underlined the necessity of, and provided a framework for ensuring that scheme managers, as a dispersed workforce, are kept on board:

- Sheltered and retirement housing schemes are no longer sidelined, isolated from their surrounding environment – they are part of a whole range of provision for older people in the local community. Scheme managers thus cannot afford to be remote from organisational policies and practices.

- Sheltered and retirement housing is now delivered within a culture of accountability and professionalism. As frontline staff, scheme managers have a key responsibility for quality service delivery. Again, contact with managers and colleagues is vital in developing an understanding of how to operate within the new culture.
- While scheme managers will have become familiar with some of the more recent issues relating to their role – for example those relating to community care and hospital discharge – others are new. In particular the requirement (outlined in the ERoSH checklist discussed on page 125) for proper briefing and training about their role under Supporting People, including needs and risk assessment, support planning, preventing abuse and promoting diversity and inclusion has significant implications for scheme managers and their service managers.

The following examples show how a range of providers ensure their dispersed workforce members have been helped to see how and why their role is changing, and are fully equipped to deliver at the front line:

Training and development

EPIC Trust holds quarterly staff briefing and training sessions. All staff have the Supporting People QAF as part of their ongoing objectives, and a monthly reporting mechanism ensures audit of practices and policy compliance.

South Somerset Homes holds training events on current issues, which have recently included abuse of vulnerable adults, risk assessments and Supporting People. In addition, 'essential skills' courses have been organised for all scheme managers to ensure that they have the relevant professional skills needed to provide an effective housing-related support service.

Central and Cecil has established quarterly sheltered team development days, in order to review service delivery, policies and procedures and working practices. Staff training is encompassed within these development days, and has recently included support planning, risk management, anti-social behaviour and harassment.

SLFHA (part of Horizon Housing Group) has developed a scheme manager training profile, listing the essential training topics for all scheme managers. Each scheme manager's personal development assessment identifies individual training needs, which feed into the annual service training plan. Training needs are met by a wide variety of development methods including study days, external training (seminars, conferences, etc) in-house training on specific topics, professional qualifications, job-shadowing, membership of working groups and visits.

→

Specific attention has been paid to ensuring that staff understand Supporting People. The whole team worked through the changes which Supporting People brought, including Support Planning. SLFHA is already reviewing the Support Plan in the light of further developments, including feedback from validation visits by Supporting People reviewers. This highlights the requirement for continuous review and improvement to services.

6.4 Promoting service users' choice and control – the key role of the service manager

Resident involvement at scheme level is discussed in detail in Chapter 2. This section focuses on the service manager's key role in:

- Supporting scheme managers to develop resident involvement at their schemes
- Ensuring opportunities are available for residents to participate more widely and at a policy level, building on the existing levels of participation developed by scheme managers. Opportunities can include tenant satisfaction surveys and service reviews.

Developing resident involvement at scheme level

Genuine involvement at scheme level is the first step towards involvement at a higher level. Since enabling and encouraging participation from diverse service users with different needs and expectations is a skilled activity, service managers must offer ongoing support to scheme managers in their efforts to reach this goal.

This is a particularly challenging area of housing management. A skills audit can show how far service managers themselves, alongside their scheme managers, may need to enhance their existing skills. Appointing specialist and experienced trainers in user participation to work with staff and residents can enhance the levels and nature of involvement and participation at all levels.

Formally constituted residents' associations are one way to facilitate formal involvement and consultation at scheme level. Retirement housing schemes can offer rented housing some lessons here, since many have had residents' associations in place for some years as a way of fulfilling the need for formal consultation on the annual service charge.

Scheme managers need support and training to ensure that residents' associations are successful, and for example do not exclude the more vulnerable service users or become dominated by the most powerful or vociferous individuals.

Poole Housing Partnership

Poole Housing Partnership has trained all its scheme managers in setting up and working with residents' associations. All 30 of its sheltered schemes now have properly constituted associations, 18 of which have dedicated Tenant Representatives. The residents' associations provide Poole residents with a clear structure for formal involvement and consultation.

However, residents' associations, even those which work well, are not enough. It is important to ensure that a range of formal and informal opportunities are available to ensure that *all* residents are encouraged and enabled to identify needs and choices, and to express their views, including those who do not participate currently or find it hard to contribute in a group (level 5 of the Ladder of Empowerment through Participation – see Chapter 2, page 31).

Good practice checklist: Supporting scheme managers with developing scheme-level involvement

- ✓ Ensure scheme managers are aware of the organisation's overall goals in respect of resident involvement, and of their own individual roles in helping to facilitate this.
- ✓ Ensure scheme managers are fully aware of the range of wider positive outcomes which stem from the process.
- ✓ Carry out a skills audit to assess training needs in this area (include service managers and scheme managers) and work with specialist trainers to improve skills in encouraging resident involvement.
- ✓ Ensure scheme managers are aware of the wide range of formal and informal methods of involving and consulting with residents, and offer relevant training to support these.
- ✓ Put in place an appropriate needs assessment and support planning process, supported by comprehensive training.
- ✓ Support scheme managers with setting up and working with residents' associations.
- ✓ Ensure scheme managers have a good knowledge of local resources and how to enable residents to access these.

Involvement at policy level

Involving residents at policy level is now a key organisational goal for all providers, and must be built into the service strategy. External funders and regulators expect providers to involve residents in planning, monitoring and reviewing how services are delivered, and to take residents' views and preferences into account when making decisions and setting targets. For example, the Housing Corporation's *Involvement Policy for the Housing Association Sector* (2004) says that housing associations should offer residents:

- Opportunities to be involved at local level or beyond if they wish
- A choice in ways of getting involved, not necessarily on a formal basis
- New choices, beyond the tried and tested methods of involvement.

To facilitate this, providers must offer a variety of different, user-friendly opportunities to maximise involvement.

As well as acting as an invaluable tool for encouraging involvement at scheme level, the ERoSH Sheltered Housing Model Support Plan also offers a good opportunity to discover individual preferences relating to involvement in wider consultation activities, as illustrated in the extract below.

Extract from ERoSH Sheltered Housing Model Support Plan 2004

Being consulted

We would very much like your views, comments, suggestions and ideas on how we could improve the service we provide to you and other service users. We have a range of consultation methods, including informal chats on daily rounds, meetings and committees.

- How would you prefer to be consulted?
- Do you want to become more involved in decision making about the sheltered housing service?
- How can we make this process accessible for you? For example if you have any language, cultural or mobility needs – how can we make it easier for you to give us your opinions and input?

Of course, some residents are too frail, opt out of, or simply ignore all attempts to involve them at any level. However, providers must not fall into the ageist trap of assuming that older people in general have no interest in such issues. Among the wide range of service users living in sheltered housing, there will be some residents who are delighted to have the opportunity to comment on services, and participate in wider decision-making, through both formal and informal involvement, as the following case studies show:

Hanover Housing Association

Hanover's experience shows that many sheltered housing residents are no less keen to be involved in decisions affecting their homes than those living in general needs housing. Older people have both the time, and a lifetime's experience to bring to the process.

Hanover promotes service users' choice and control in a range of ways, for example:

- At scheme level, residents are able to influence service charges by working with the estate manager in the selection of gardening and cleaning contractors.
- All schemes can elect a resident representative to attend quarterly Regional Forums, meeting with senior regional staff to discuss policy development and monitor performance.
- A residents' council meets as a sub-committee of the group board, and four residents sit on the housing management committee, another sub-committee of the group board. There is one resident place on the group board, ensuring that the residents' viewpoint is represented at the highest level of decision-making.

Wales and West Housing Association

Wales and West has enabled a group of residents to represent their peers from across Wales. Quarterly meetings are held at various venues, and topics on the agenda include Supporting People, the current ongoing review, and the action plan contained within the residents' compact.

Rhondda Cynon Taff County Borough Council

Rhondda Cynon Taff's sheltered housing tenants are represented on the local tenants' and residents' federation, and sheltered housing staff have had training from the local tenant participation officer to help them undertake this new aspect of their role.

Involving residents in determining what they want from the service helps the organisation prioritise the issues that are important to residents. Once the vision is determined, and service aims and objectives identified, residents can be involved in monitoring delivery of the service which they have helped to shape.

Swaythling Housing Society

In the course of gaining accreditation with the CSHS Code of Practice for Sheltered Housing, Swaythling worked with sheltered housing residents to devise a mission statement, and involved them in setting clear objectives for the sheltered service.

Swaythling invited representatives from each of the Society's seven sheltered schemes to a meeting to discuss:

- What did residents want from the Society?
- What was the most important thing that the Society did for sheltered scheme residents?
- What could the Society do differently?
- What should be the Society's sheltered housing mission statement?

Through this consultation exercise, the organisation was able to identify what residents thought of the service, and how it could improve. A mission statement for Swaythling's sheltered housing service was also devised and adopted, encompassing the key elements that now underpin Swaythling's service:

> *"Providing high quality, good value homes with a friendly community atmosphere and stimulating activities for residents".*

Tenant satisfaction surveys

Tenant satisfaction surveys are an established mechanism for assessing the standard and quality of services provided, and are integral to improving performance. Since many existing surveys are inadequate for sheltered housing, the three largest sheltered housing providers in England commissioned the University of Salford to develop a tenant satisfaction measurement for sheltered housing. The Housing Corporation supported the project through its Innovation and Good Practice Grant programme.

The format of the eventual questionnaire was created through pilot work with service users, who shaped the type, scope and format of the questions. Two versions of the questionnaire are included in the document – one for face-to-face meetings and the other for use in a postal survey. The main preference of older people was for face-to-face interviews – this was the case with all the BME tenants, Extra Care tenants and those with visual impairments who took part in the pilot. The authors of the project therefore strongly discourage the use of the postal survey format unless the intended users are 'young' elders.

During the pilot a number of themes emerged:

- Although satisfaction levels appeared high, many respondents added a proviso that, while they were satisfied during office hours when the scheme manager was available, there were concerns about cover outside these hours.
- There was a degree of cynicism around consultation, as many respondents felt that there was no 'genuine consultation'.
- Security was an important issue, though crime was not seen as a significant problem.
- Respondents felt uneasy about making negative comments in relation to scheme managers.

The final guide helps providers implement tenant satisfaction surveys among sheltered housing tenants. It gives detailed guidance on the various stages of implementing a satisfaction survey through a partnership approach with older people, including:

- The resource implications of undertaking satisfaction surveys
- The advantages and disadvantages of undertaking the study in-house or employing outside consultants
- The role of the scheme manager (they should *not* conduct the survey)
- Producing a research brief
- Choosing an appropriate method for conducting the survey, bearing in mind the characteristics of the sheltered housing residents
- Running focus group discussion
- Strategies for maximising response rates
- Sampling techniques and sample sizes
- Strategies for analyzing the data
- Providing feedback to different audiences.

■ Resident involvement in service reviews

The process of service review, and the toolkits and support available to service managers and staff are comprehensively covered in Chapter 5. Service managers should be aware that the process of service change and review offers a further key opportunity for resident involvement. Residents can and should be fully involved in changes which affect them.

Testway Housing

Testway Housing undertook a Best Value review of the warden service, including considering the way out-of-hours cover was provided to clients.

→

Having analysed their out-of-hours calls, Testway found that the majority were not 'real' emergencies at all. They were either accidental, or required the mobile warden to give access to the scheme, or needed the emergency services who could be contacted directly on behalf of the resident concerned. Testway felt that the money spent on providing an out-of-hours service might be better spent in other ways to benefit sheltered housing clients. However they wanted to ensure residents and other stakeholders understood all the issues and had the opportunity to participate in the decision.

Testway organised a comprehensive consultation programme, using a wide range of methods including surveys, focus groups with existing and potential customers, and telephone or face-to-face interviews with individuals. Clients were offered a range of four options for service change, and were asked to give their first and second choices in each case.

Clients were given full feedback on the decisions made as a result of their choices, and throughout the change process received updates through a special newsletter. Six months on, they were surveyed to determine customer satisfaction with the changes.

Activities such as these, where service users can clearly see the influence they have had on policies and practices, go some way towards ensuring that consultation is genuine, and not simply a box-ticking exercise carried out by providers. Service users want to know what has happened or changed as a result of their input, and providers need to build this feedback into consultation processes.

■ Clear service information

To promote choice and control, residents must understand what services are available to them. The needs assessment and support planning process frequently shows that residents have not been receiving services to which they are entitled, largely because they did not know about them.

The service manager must ensure that all residents are fully aware of the support they can access on-scheme, and the support which their scheme manager can facilitate for them from other agencies. Clarifying their entitlements has a further important benefit, that of ensuring residents, and their relatives and carers, are clear about the boundaries of the scheme manager's role.

Central and Cecil

Central and Cecil's scheme agreements set out in a very clear and transparent way what services tenants can expect to receive from Central and Cecil, and how to access services and support at local scheme level.

Housing 21

Housing 21 promises all sheltered housing residents that, on all schemes, they will arrange access to, or directly offer, the following services:

- Assistance to users to get out and about
- Shopping and cleaning services
- Welfare benefits advice
- Access to personal care services
- Physical and mental health activities taking place on the scheme.

This Service Promise was developed through listening to and acting upon the views of residents, who see the availability of this range of services as an improvement to their quality of life.

Swaythling Housing Society

Swaythling wanted to ensure their residents received all the support that was available, and asked them to complete a tick-list indicating their awareness, and take-up of services. From the responses it was clear that not everyone knew about all that their Scheme Manager could do for them. A list was devised detailing these services, which was sent to all residents and which is now also kept on the notice board in each scheme:

Your Scheme Manager will do all this for you, all you need to do is ask:

- *Help you set up and maintain your home and tenancy/lease*
- *Enable you to develop domestic or life skills, in liaison with other agencies (if you would like this)*
- *Help support you to become part of the community and to access local community organisations*
- *Provide advice*
- *Help you gain access to other services*
- *Help you establish social contacts and activities*
- *Support you to establish your personal safety and security*
- *Consider your health and wellbeing*
- *Help find you other accommodation if you would like/need to move*
- *Regularly check that your community alarms (pull-cords) are working*
- *Help you maintain the safety and security of your home.*

CDS Housing

CDS Housing's recently revised residents' handbook focuses on the changing role of the scheme manager (called Community Support Officer at CDS) and the introduction of Supporting People. The handbook clarifies roles and responsibilities and provides a useful guide to living in CDS sheltered accommodation. As a supplement, CDS also produced a leaflet *Sheltered Accommodation – A Relatives' Guide* which sets out clear boundaries for the role of the Community Support Officer. Sheltered tenants and staff were involved in developing both these documents.

❑ 6.5 Resolving disputes within sheltered and retirement housing

Conflict and disputes can and do arise within sheltered and retirement housing, and it is important that service managers offer full support to scheme managers where this occurs. Such conflict can occur between individual residents, between residents and the scheme manager, or between residents and the organisation itself. Within sheltered and retirement housing, such conflict is frequently heightened because of the close nature of the community, and where a resident scheme manager is involved the situation can become extremely stressful, since, for the staff member, there is no escape from the situation at the end of the working day. Prompt and clear action on the part of the service manager is necessary in all conflict situations to avoid escalation.

Mediation by an impartial external organisation is becoming increasingly popular as a way of resolving disputes, in sheltered housing and elsewhere. It is cost-effective, fast and allows the parties involved in the dispute to determine their own future by drawing up an agreement between themselves with the aid of mediators as facilitators.

Mediation differs from litigation, ombudsman referral and arbitration whereby a third party makes the decisions for those involved, which inevitably leads to a winner/loser situation. Mediation, on the other hand, encourages all parties involved in the dispute to be 'winners' and consequently results in a more harmonious and enduring outcome. Mediators help people identify their needs, clarify issues, explore situations and negotiate an agreement. The parties in the dispute, not the mediator, decide the terms of this agreement. Mediation usually focuses on future rather than past behaviour.

The specialist service, AIMS, offers impartial information, advice and mediation for any person who lives in or is involved in providing sheltered or retirement housing. The emphasis throughout the work of AIMS is on dispute prevention and resolution. Many providers now see AIMS as a crucial resource and key partner which can assist with resolving specific disputes, and offers training in conflict and dispute resolution techniques. See the AIMS website for more details, www.ageconcern.org.uk/aims

AIMS mediation – typical stages in the process

- Once people have agreed to mediate, AIMS asks everyone to sign a formal agreement which sets out the terms of the mediation and gives the process its confidentiality.
- The mediation is usually held on neutral territory, but in any event, the location is decided, like everything else in mediation, by agreement between the parties. Depending on the circumstances, it is usual for the parties to meet separately first with the mediator and then together. The mediator will remind everyone of the principles of mediation and each party will have an opportunity to give their account of the dispute without interruption.
- Moving on in the mediation will usually mean that the parties will be working with the mediator separately and together to explore solutions to the problems.
- Towards the end of the mediation the mediator will usually ask the parties to come together again for further discussions. The mediator will help to write up the agreements which have been made. Everyone is then asked to sign the agreement and the mediation session is closed.
- AIMS keeps a record of the agreement but no other records of the meeting are kept. The AIMS administrator types up the agreement and sends it to everyone within 48 hours of the mediation.

There are times when the procedure may be different, depending on individual circumstances, and AIMS can offer advice on how best to use mediation.

❑ 6.6 Conclusions

This chapter has examined the role of the service manager in ensuring the effective operation of today's sheltered housing service, and enabling it to respond to the challenges which the next few years will inevitably bring.

The service must be flexible. It must have a clear vision and aims, which will enable it to meet the needs and aspirations of older people, both its current and projected future service users. Frontline staff must be enabled to keep up with the current pace of change taking place within sheltered housing. As key players in the delivery of change, they must be kept informed, supported and trained to ensure that they understand and are fully able to carry out the new tasks required of them.

The service manager is crucial to this process. Their role in devising the service vision and strategy and ensuring its implementation, developing and maintaining strategic partnerships, motivating and supporting scheme-based staff, ensuring high quality service delivery, and liaising with service users, ensuring their views are heard at all levels, cannot be underestimated.

As the interface between the strategic and operational aspects of the service, the service manager is pivotal in pulling together all the key elements in order to 'make it happen'.

Good practice checklist: Managing the sheltered housing service today and for the future

- ✓ The service must be flexible.
- ✓ Service managers must lead on the development of a service vision and strategy, and ensure its implementation.
- ✓ The service vision, strategy and aims must enable the service to meet the needs and aspirations of older people, both current and future service users.
- ✓ The needs of a dispersed workforce must be fully taken into account in all aspects of service management.
- ✓ Frontline staff must be kept abreast of changes taking place within sheltered housing.
- ✓ Frontline staff must be kept informed, supported and trained to carry out the new role and tasks.
- ✓ Service managers must develop and maintain local strategic partnerships across housing, health and social care.
- ✓ Service managers must ensure they themselves, together with their staff team, have the necessary skills to work effectively in the new climate (skills audits can help here) and must ensure specialist training is available where needed.
- ✓ Service managers must ensure formal and informal consultation takes place with service users, ensuring their views are heard at all levels.
- ✓ Service managers should make use of the available toolkits to assess tenant satisfaction and to undertake service reviews, and should involve residents in the review process.
- ✓ Service managers should ensure feedback is given to residents on the outcomes of their involvement.
- ✓ The services and support that residents can expect must be made clear to service users, their relatives and carers.
- ✓ Service managers should take prompt action whenever disputes occur, supporting scheme-based staff and calling in specialist mediation services to assist when required.

CHAPTER 7

PREPARING FOR THE FUTURE

This chapter draws together the themes explored throughout this Guide, summarising:

- **What** sheltered housing offers
- **Who** sheltered housing is for
- **How** the sheltered housing service can ensure it is equipped to meet changing patterns of use and demand, now and in the future, via a focus on:
  - service users
  - staff
  - strategy
  - service structure and delivery
  - buildings.

Sheltered housing has had to rapidly develop, grow and change in response to a wide range of influences in recent years, including:

- Central and local government initiatives and strategies which place older people centre stage
- The increasingly competitive climate within housing from the late 1990s onwards, with an emphasis on quality and accountability
- The regulatory, inspection and contract framework within which sheltered housing now operates
- Reviews of service relevance, outcomes, demand and quality within sheltered housing introduced through the Supporting People programme
- New requirements such as needs and risk assessment, support planning and protection from abuse.

These factors have all contributed to the realisation among providers that the traditional approaches to managing sheltered housing are not appropriate for the 21st century. The key tasks for providers are to:

- Deliver good quality services which meet the needs of existing residents
- Ensure that they are ready to meet future challenges as the purpose and remit of sheltered housing continues to change.

The best providers are already achieving these tasks, and there is much that others can learn from them.

❑ 7.1 What sheltered housing offers

Providers must embrace the ever-widening vision of **what** sheltered housing offers, and promote it to others. Sheltered and retirement housing can provide:

- Self-contained, easy to manage, non-institutional accommodation
- Security – provided by support staff and by design features of the building, including assistive technology
- Peace of mind, and help in emergencies
- A supportive environment – provided by support staff and other residents
- Company and companionship
- Independence
- Prevention of depression, loneliness, anxiety and falls
- Empowerment, involvement, participation and active citizenship
- Social inclusion
- A place for leisure, lifelong learning and intergenerational links
- A venue for home care and day care
- A resource/hub for the wider community
- An alternative to residential care.

❑ 7.2 Who sheltered housing is for

Providers and stakeholders are revising their original perceptions of **who** sheltered housing is for, and are looking at how services can meet the needs of this diverse group. Sheltered housing is for:

- Older people with housing needs and/or support needs
- Older people with low, medium or high support and/or care needs
- Mentally frail older people, including those with dementia
- Physically frail older people
- Older people with sensory impairments
- Black and minority ethnic older people
- Older people with learning disabilities
- Older people with alcohol and drug dependence problems
- Older lesbians and gay men
- Older people who have been homeless
- People with some of the above needs who have not necessarily reached old age.

❑ 7.3 How sheltered housing can prepare to meet future demands

This Guide has demonstrated **how** organisations are meeting the changing pattern of needs, and encourages sheltered housing providers to learn from each other's successes, regardless of where they are located within the sector.

A set of key good practice principles is set out by theme below; providers which achieve these are not only delivering a quality service to their residents of today, but are also are in a good position to meet the further changing needs of tomorrow.

Good practice principles checklist: Service users

- ✓ Are offered support based on clearly identified needs and intended outcomes
- ✓ Have diverse needs catered for, which may include higher level needs than 'traditional' sheltered housing tenants and could include those associated with: learning disabilities, mental health problems, drug and alcohol misuse, ex street homeless
- ✓ Are offered flexible (rather than a 'one size fits all') service provision which may include a menu of options
- ✓ Have the opportunity to be part of and contribute to a safe and supportive community
- ✓ Understand clearly the service provision, their entitlements and the service parameters
- ✓ Have a range of opportunities to comment on services and to become involved at strategic as well as operational levels
- ✓ Are empowered, within a climate of openness and accountability
- ✓ Have a range of opportunities for inclusion and involvement
- ✓ May not live in a designated sheltered housing scheme but in the wider community.

Good practice principles checklist: Staff

- ✓ Are knowledgeable, skilled and well trained
- ✓ Are supervised and supported by specialist managers
- ✓ Have up-to-date job descriptions and are recruited on matched person specifications

→

- ✓ Work within clear boundaries, guidelines, codes of conduct, regularly updated manuals of procedures, policies and guidance
- ✓ Are customer-focused
- ✓ Promote service user involvement at scheme and community level in a range of ways
- ✓ Are responsive to service users' needs and wider aspirations
- ✓ Are open to working with a wide range of service users
- ✓ Are aware of funding, outcome and quality requirements
- ✓ Are sensitive to cultural, ethnic, lifestyle, religious and diversity issues
- ✓ Are open to working outside the traditional sheltered scheme boundaries.

Good practice principles checklist: Service strategy

- ✓ Is linked to and congruent with the local authority older people's strategy and the local Supporting People strategy on older people's services
- ✓ Is focused on meeting needs of older people in the community, not just those in providers' properties
- ✓ Addresses identified local demographic changes over the next 10 years and beyond – tenure, BME etc
- ✓ Is based on shared visions of services for older people
- ✓ Lettings policies:
  - balance principles of need and choice
  - ensure effective advertising and publicity of schemes and services
  - address and resolve tensions between traditional allocations to sheltered housing with new directions sought by Supporting People teams (eg the 'balanced community' of those with high, moderate and low support needs vs support services focused only on those with higher needs, with preventative services given low priority)
- ✓ Is based on shared targets and performance indicators
- ✓ Identifies and minimises the risks associated with uncertain support revenue funding
- ✓ Is based on a range of models which include: a menu approach, a team approach, a non-building focused approach
- ✓ Uses language which can be understood by other agencies
- ✓ Evidences service user input in drafting and ratification.

Good practice principles checklist: Service structure and delivery

- ✓ The sheltered housing service has strong, focused and knowledgeable management, which takes account of the needs of a dispersed workforce
- ✓ A positive emphasis on diversity underpins the service
- ✓ Service provision and delivery are supported by continuous improvement targets
- ✓ Regular service and scheme reviews take place, ensuring that the environment is safe and healthy, the service is demonstrably high quality and appropriate, and the buildings are fit for the future
- ✓ Opportunities for service user involvement at operational and strategic level are promoted
- ✓ Partnership working takes place at operational and strategic levels and with a range of stakeholders
- ✓ Clear guidelines and regular support and training for scheme based staff are in place
- ✓ Can respond to increasing numbers of service users opting for Direct Payments or individual budgets
- ✓ Can respond to commissioners' shifting emphasis from solely scheme-based services to floating support and outreach work.

Good practice principles checklist: Buildings

- ✓ Provide well maintained, secure, self-contained accommodation
- ✓ Have a lift
- ✓ Are well located
- ✓ Meet mobility and decent homes standards
- ✓ Have a separate communal lounge with own facilities
- ✓ Have a non-institutional appearance
- ✓ Feature appropriate, inexpensive adaptations and assistive technology, available as needed
- ✓ Are audited against regulators' standards for older people's housing
- ✓ Remodelling proposals take account of existing provision in the local area, local older peoples' strategies, social and demographic influences, aspirations of 'younger' older people, diversity, the need for Extra Care provision in the area etc
- ✓ Future remodelling/new build is consistent with rising expectations of future generations of older people (eg desire for two bedrooms and computer terminals).

Change is the only certainty for sheltered and retirement housing providers. Cultural, demographic, policy and legislative changes will continue into the foreseeable future. It has been the intention of this Guide to assist staff at all levels by outlining the impact of these changes on sheltered housing, and by demonstrating that there is a wealth of existing good practice which can be copied and adapted to help 'future proof' the service to which they and the authors are so passionately committed.

APPENDIX 1

REFERENCES AND SOURCES OF FURTHER INFORMATION

Chapter 1: The Changing Context

References

Audit Commission (1998) *Home Alone – the role of housing in community care*

DETR/DH (2001) *Quality and Choice for Older People's Housing: a strategic framework*

Department of Health (2001) *National Service Framework for Older People*

Department of Health (2005) Green Paper: *Independence, Well-being and Choice – Our vision for the future of social care for adults in England*

Housing Corporation (2002) *Housing for Older People: The Corporation's housing policy for older people*

Housing Corporation (2003) *Strategy for Housing Older People in England*

Housing Corporation (2004) Circular 03/04 *Definitions of housing association supported housing and housing for older people*

ODPM/Department of Health/Housing Corporation (2003) *Preparing Older People's Strategies: Linking housing to health, social care and other local strategies*

Opinion Research Business (2003) *A Better Life: Private Sheltered Housing and Independent Living for Older People*

Scottish Federation of Housing Associations (2005) Discussion Paper: *Sheltered Housing's Future*

Welsh Assembly Government (2003) *The Strategy for Older People in Wales*

National Assembly for Wales, Social Justice and Regeneration Committee (2004) *Housing for Older People*

ODPM, Social Exclusion Unit (2005) *Excluded Older People*

DWP (2005) *Opportunity Age: Meeting the challenge of ageing in the 21st century*

Sources of further information

National Statistical Office www.statistics.gov.uk

Age Concern England www.ageconcern.org.uk

Department of Health www.dh.gov.uk

Office of the Deputy Prime Minister, Supporting People website www.spkweb.org.uk

Extra Care – see references and sources of further information for Chapter 4

Chapter 2: The Ever-changing Role of the Scheme Manager

References

Sussex Gerontology Workshop (2004) *A Care Team for Sheltered/Retirement Housing*, University of Sussex, Brighton

Fisk, Malcolm (2003) *Social Alarms to Telecare – older people's services in transition*, Policy Press

Bradley, David, Brownsell, Simon and Porteous, Jeremy (2003) *Assistive Technology and Telecare*, Policy Press

Sources of further information

CSHS (formerly the Centre for Sheltered Housing Studies) – sheltered housing focused training, education, good practice development, short courses, conferences, consultancy, and the Code of Practice for Sheltered Housing
Website: www.cshs.co.uk Tel: 01905 21155
Email: cshs@cornwall.ac.uk

Chartered Instititute of Housing – the professional organisation for people working in housing – offers a range of services including: good practice and policy information; training and conferences; and educational courses to study for a recognised qualification at college or through distance learning
Website: www.cih.org Tel: 024 7685 1700

Department of Health – information on health structures and strategies
Website: www.dh.gov.uk

ERoSH: the National Consortium for Sheltered Housing – representative body for sheltered housing providers: best practice, publications and leaflets, awareness campaigns
Website: www.shelteredhousing.org Tel/fax: 01249 654249
Email: info@shelteredhousing.org

Harrow Judgment/Working Time Directive – CSHS FAQ sheet (see CSHS above)

National Wardens Association – support for scheme managers working with clients in sheltered housing
Email: nwa@assocmanagement.co.uk Tel: 01989 566699

Sussex Gerontology Network – discussion forum, exploring issues relating to older people and housing/health/social issues, and publication of occasional reports: c/o Professor Peter Lloyd, School of Social Sciences and Cultural Studies, University of Sussex, Brighton BN1 9SN

Chapter 3: Working with Diversity

References

Housing Corporation (2003) *Strategy for Housing Older People in England*
Website: www.housingcorp.gov.uk Tel: 0845 230 7000
Email: enquiries@housingcorp.gsx.gov.uk

ERoSH – sheltered housing information leaflets in a range of community languages
Website: www.shelteredhousing.org Tel/fax: 01249 654249
Email: info@shelteredhousing.org

Hubbard, Ruth and Rossington, John (1995) *As We Grow Older – a study of the housing and support needs of older lesbians and gay men*, Polari HA

Equally Different (2003) Opening Doors in Thanet (ODIT) PO Box 382, Ramsgate CT11 9XR

Communities Scotland (2005) Research Report 54 *The housing and support needs of older lesbian, gay, bisexual and transgender (LGBT) people in Scotland*

Communities Scotland (2005) *Housing options for older LGBT people in Scotland*

Department of Health Fact Sheet *Extra Care Housing Options for Older People with Functional Mental Health Problems*

Audit Commission (2004) *Implementing Telecare*
audit-publications@twoten.pres.net Tel 0800 502030

Department of Health Integrating Community Equipment Services (2004) *Getting Started in Telecare*, www.icesdoh.org

Kitwood, T, Buckland, S and Petre, T (1995) *Brighter Futures: A report on research into provisions for people with dementia in residential homes, nursing homes and sheltered housing*, Anchor Housing

Kitwood, T and Benson, S (eds) (1995) *People with dementia in sheltered housing* published in 'The new culture of dementia care', Hawker Publications

Help the Aged and HACT (2002) *Sheltered housing and the resettlement of older homeless people*, available from info@helptheaged.org.uk Tel: 0207 239 1946

Sources of further information

Federation of Black Housing Organisations (FBHO)
Website: www.fbho.org.uk Tel: 020 8533 705

Alzheimers Society – care and research charity offering information for people with dementia and their families and carers
Website: www.alzheimers.org.uk

Dementia North – the Dementia Services Development Centre (DSDC) for the Northern and Yorkshire regions – a partnership between the University of Northumbria and the Dementia North Trust
Website – access via the University of Northumberland website: www.northumbria.ac.uk. Tel: 0191 215 6110
Email: hs.dementianorth@northumbria.ac.uk

Dementia Voice – the Dementia Services Development Centre (DSDC) for the South West of England
Website: www.dementia-voice.org.uk
Email: office@dementia-voice.org.uk

(DSDCs are a national network across the UK, supported by the Department of Health, which offer support, research, consultancy, publications, etc)

EAC (Elderly Accommodation Counsel)
Website: www.housingcare.org Tel: 020 7820 1343
Email: enquiries@eac.org.uk

Department of Health Housing Learning and Improvement Network (LIN)
Housing LIN Factsheets and case studies:
Factsheet 3: *New provisions for older people with learning disabilities*
Factsheet 5: *Assistive technology in extra care housing*
Factsheet 7: *Private sector provision of extra care housing*
Factsheet 15: *Extra care housing options for older people with functional mental health problems*
Case Study 3: *Least-use assistive technology in dementia care*
All available from: www.changeagentteam.org.uk

RNIB – information, support and advice in relation to the 2 million people with sight problems in the UK
Website: www.rnib.org.uk

RNID – information support, advice and representation for the 9 million deaf and hard-of-hearing people in the UK.
Website: www.rnid.org.uk

St Mungo's www.mungos.org

Willow Housing (2004) *Anti-Social Behaviour in Sheltered Housing Policy* Tel: 020 8782 5496

Home Connections website www.home-connections.co.uk
See also www.virtualtours360.net

Chapter 4: Working in Partnership

References

Integrated Care Network (2004) *Integrated working: a guide* www.integratedcarenetwork.gov.uk

Peter Fletcher Associates *Briefing paper on NSF for older people and the implications for housing organisations* www.peterfletcherassociates.co.uk

Fletcher, P, Riseborough, M et al (1999) *Citizenship and Services in Older Age: The Strategic Role of Very Sheltered Housing*, Housing 21

Audit Commission (1998) *Home Alone – the role of housing in community care*

Chartered Institute of Housing in Scotland (2005) *Essential Connections: Linking housing, health and social care*

DETR/DH (1997) *Making partnerships work in community care – a guide for practitioners in housing, health and social services*

Department of Health (2001) *National Service Framework for Older People*

Opinion Research Business (2003) *A Better Life: Private Sheltered Housing and Independent Living for Older People*

Brooks, Liz et al (2003) *Care and Support in Very Sheltered Housing, Counsel and Care* www.counselandcare.org.uk

Sources of further information

Department of Health Housing Learning & Improvement Network (LIN), part of the Social Care Change Agent Team
Website: www.changeagentteam.org.uk/housing
Email: housinglin@eac.org.uk

Department of Health (2004) *Extra Care Housing for Older People: an introduction for commissioners*, obtainable via www.changeagentteam.org.uk/housing

Department of Health (2004) *Developing and Implementing Local Extra Care Housing Strategies*, obtainable via www.changeagentteam.org.uk/housing

Department of Health – information on health structures and strategies – see website www.dh.qov.uk

Chartered Institute of Housing (2004) *Good Practice Briefing 29: Housing and Health*

Integrated Care Network – advice on delivering services using a partnership approach, moving beyond co-ordination to integration
Website: www.integratedcarenetwork.gov.uk

Elderly Accommodation Counsel (EAC) – maintains a national database of all forms of accommodation for older people
Website: www.housingcare.org Tel: 020 7820 1343
Email: enquiries@eac.org.uk

Kings Fund reading list on Intermediate Care (January 2005)
www.kingsfund.org.uk

Spencer, Sheila and Fletcher, Peter (2002) *Working with the new health and social care agenda* (2nd edition), National Housing Federation www.housing.org.uk

ERoSH (2004) – checklists for health and social services
Website: www.shelteredhousing.org Tel/fax: 01249 654249
Email: info@shelteredhousing.org

Housing for Older People Alliance HOPA – via 6 member organisations:

- Advice Information and Mediation Service (AIMS)
  www.ageconcern.org.uk/aims aims@ace.org.uk 0208 765 7465

- Association of Retirement Housing Managers (ARHM) www.arhm.org enquiries@arhm.org 020 7463 0660
- Association of Social Alarms Providers (ASAP) www.asap-uk.org info@asap-uk.org 01634 846209
- CSHS (formerly the Centre for Sheltered Housing Studies) www.cshs.co.uk cshs@cornwall.ac.uk 01905 21155
- Elderly Accommodation Counsel (EAC) www.housingcare.org enquiries@eac.org.uk 0207 820 1343
- ERoSH (formerly Emerging Role of Sheltered Housing) www.shelteredhousing.org info@shelteredhousing.org 01249 654249

Hairnet: www.hairnet.org 0870 241 5091

Chapter 5: Quality, Standards and Performance

References

ODPM, Supporting People website www.spkweb.org.uk helpline 020 7944 2556

Hanover Housing Association (2005) *Protection of vulnerable adults – Operational guidance, policies, procedures and supporting information* available from www.hanover.org.uk price £25

Sources of further information

Local Supporting People strategies: see local authority websites

Audit Commission – inspection reports, KLOEs www.audit-commission.gov.uk

CSHS (formerly the Centre for Sheltered Housing Studies)
Website: www.cshs.co.uk Tel: 01905 21155
Email: cshs@cornwall.ac.uk

Association of Retirement Housing Managers (ARHM)
Website: www.arhm.org Tel: 020 7463 0660
Email: enquiries@arhm.org

Association of Social Alarms Providers (ASAP)
Website: www.asap-uk.org Tel: 08700 434052
Email: info@asap-uk.org

Housemark www.housemark.co.uk

Housing Quality Network www.hqnetwork.org.uk

Secta Starfish www.sectastarfish.co.uk

Northern Housing Consortium www.northern-consortium.org.uk

Elderly Accommodation Counsel (EAC)
Website: www.housingcare.org Tel: 020 7820 1343
Email: enquiries@eac.org.uk

Care and Repair England
Website: www.careandrepair-england.org.uk Tel/fax: 0115 950 6500

References

Thompson, L and Page, D (1999) *Effective Sheltered Housing: A Gu*
Chartered Institute of Housing

CSHS (formerly the Centre for Sheltered Housing Studies)
Website: www.cshs.co.uk T. ..1155
Email: cshs@cornwall.ac.uk

ERoSH (2004) *Checklist for Sheltered and Retirement Housing Providers*
ERoSH (2004) *Sheltered Housing Model Support Plan*
Website: www.shelteredhousing.org Tel/fax: 01249 654249
Email: info@shelteredhousing.org

Housing Corporation (2004) *Involvement policy for the housing association sector*
Website: www.housingcorp.gov.uk Tel: 0845 230 7000
Email: enquiries@housingcorp.gsx.gov.uk

Savory, J and Sodhi, D (2002) *University of Salford Tenant Satisfaction Measurement for Sheltered Housing*, Housing Corporation, Anchor Trust, Housing 21 and Hanover Housing Association, available from Lynda Borthwick, Hanover Housing Association, Tel: 01784 446010 lynda.borthwick@hanover.org.uk

Sources of further information

AIMS – Advice Information and Mediation Services, a specialist Age Concern England service offering impartial advice and information to residents of sheltered and retirement housing
Website: www.ageconcern.org.uk/aims Tel: 0208 765 7465
Email: aims@ace.org.uk

Elderly Accommodation Counsel (EAC) – helps older people to make informed choices about housing and care options. Maintains a national database of all forms of accommodation for older people
Website: www.housingcare.org Tel: 020 7820 1343
Email: enquiries@eac.org.uk

Strategy development: Housing LIN workbook and video on CD-rom, *Strategic Moves: Thinking, Planning and Working Differently*
www.changeagentteam.org.uk

APPENDIX 2

GLOSSARY

Accreditation
The process by which a service provider is approved by the Supporting People Commissioning Body (see below) to deliver Supporting People services.

ALMO
Arms Length Management Organisation – a company set up by a local authority to manage and improve all or part of its housing stock. The company is owned by the local authority and operates under the terms of a management agreement between the authority and the ALMO. High performing ALMOs can spend more on the properties they manage.

Audit Commission Housing Inspectorate
Carries out inspections of housing services provided by local authorities and housing associations. Also inspects Administering Authorities (see below) to ensure that they are implementing the Supporting People programme in accordance with ODPM requirements and guidance.

Best Value
The requirement of social housing providers to review and improve services in consultation with service users and other stakeholders.

BME elders
Older members of black and minority ethnic groups.

'Category 1' and 'Category 2' sheltered housing
Former descriptors of sheltered housing, no longer in official use – replaced by Housing Corporation definitions of housing for older people, see below.

Contracts
The support service in rented sheltered housing was previously funded through housing benefit and is now provided through Supporting People via a contract between each provider and the Supporting People Administering Authority in the local area. Existing providers received an interim contract on 1 April 2003 subject to the outcome of the first service reviews (see below).

CSHS
Formerly the Centre for Sheltered Housing Studies. Provides sheltered housing focused training, education, good practice development, short courses, conferences, consultancy, and the Code of Practice for Sheltered Housing.

Decent Homes Standard
A government standard which includes modern kitchens and bathrooms, central heating and double glazing. Each home should also be in good repair and have modern heating and insulation systems. All social housing is required to meet the Decent Homes Standard by 2010 (see also Options Appraisal, below).

ERoSH
Originally the Emerging Role of the Warden Project. Now the National Consortium for Sheltered Housing – representative body for sheltered housing providers, delivering best practice, publications and leaflets, and awareness campaigns.

Extra Care
Purpose-built schemes or those which have been remodelled to provide a barrier-free environment which facilitates mobility and access for frail older people. Such schemes offer a sheltered housing style model of service delivery, in which the key support element, traditionally defined as a 'warden type' service, is available alongside a domiciliary care service, as well as a personal care element. Extra Care schemes may be rented or leasehold. Some Extra Care schemes offer special facilities for those suffering from mental frailty and dementia. Names for this type of service provision may include Category 2½, Very Sheltered, Assisted Living, Frail Elders units, etc.

Housing Corporation
The government agency which registers, regulates and funds over 2,000 social landlords in England. Since the introduction of the Supporting People programme, matters relating to the support service of sheltered housing are regulated by local Supporting People Administering Authorities.

Housing Corporation definitions of housing for older people
Three definitions of housing for older people:

- All special design features
- Some special design features
- Designated supported housing for older people (ie buildings with no special design features).

Tenants in the first two groups should have access to support services, as need arises, to enable them to live in the property for the rest of their lifetimes.

Housing for Older People Alliance (HOPA)
An alliance of currently six national organisations whose key purposes include promoting, regulating, and/or advising on sheltered and retirement housing (see Chapter 4, section 4.8 for further details).

Intergenerational work
Intergenerational approaches bring people of different ages together in order to promote greater understanding and respect between generations and to help build healthier communities. Intergenerational work is inclusive, building on the positive resources that different generations have to offer each other and their communities. It is an effective way to address a number of issues, many of them key government priorities such as building active communities, promoting citizenship, regenerating neighbourhoods and addressing inequality.

Intermediate Care
Intermediate Care is the term used for the range of short-term, patient focused services designed to promote and maintain the independence of older people otherwise facing inappropriate admissions to hospital, long-term care or prolonged stays in hospital. Methods for achieving this aim include: supported discharge, rapid response and day rehabilitation.

KLOEs
Key Lines of Enquiry – a set of questions and statements which provide consistent criteria used by the Audit Commission for assessing and measuring the effectiveness and efficiency of housing related services.

Leasehold
A form of tenure which gives the owner possession of the property for a substantial period of time which is clearly defined in the lease agreement.

NHS National Service Framework for Older People
Aims to improve standards of care for older people. The framework includes eight national standards and an additional appendix on medicines. Health authorities and primary care trusts will be judged against how they deliver these standards in their local areas. A number of the standards are also incorporated into national targets for the NHS and social services departments.

ODPM
Office of the Deputy Prime Minister – the government department whose responsibilities include the Supporting People programme.

Options appraisal
When a local authority is considering which option will enable it to achieve the Decent Homes Standard it must first conduct an options appraisal. This involves investigating all the options for housing investment and working out the costs and

benefits of each. Local authorities must involve tenants fully in the options appraisal process and seek their views on the local priorities and outcomes. Tenant participation is essential to the options appraisal procedure, as this will help ensure that any scheme meets the needs of the local community.

Performance Indicators (PIs)
Statistics and data (that may be quantitative or qualitative) that is analysed to measure organisational activity. PIs may focus on inputs, processes, outputs or outcomes. They are a key feature of the Supporting People programme and of other regulatory systems.

Quality Assessment Framework (QAF)
The QAF is a key element of the Supporting People programme, requiring support providers to demonstrate the achievement of defined standards of service – see Chapter 5, section 5.1 for details.

Retirement housing
Within this Guide, this term is used to describe leasehold housing schemes (where it is necessary to distinguish between this and rented sheltered housing in the text). Frequently known as 'private retirement housing', it comprises small, easy to manage homes which meet the needs of older owner-occupiers, specifically built for sale to this client group. Accommodation is sold on long leases.

Scheme manager
The most generally used term for the member of staff who co-ordinates and manages a particular sheltered housing scheme (or schemes), working directly with service users in order to facilitate their independence. Previously known as 'warden', though this title is generally felt to be outdated. They may be resident or non-resident in the scheme. Some organisations use other terms eg estate manager, court manager or sheltered housing officer for this role.

Service reviews
Service reviews are undertaken by Supporting People Administering Authorities, in order to decide whether the contract (see above) should be renewed, and if so, on what terms. Reviews of all provision should be completed by March 2006.

Sheltered housing
Within this Guide, this term is used to describe a wide range of housing for rent that is aimed at older and/or disabled or (increasingly) other vulnerable people. It includes grouped housing with a resident or visiting scheme manager, flats or bungalows that may be built in a block, or on one site, or dispersed. Accommodation is self-contained and easy to manage. Categories that were formerly used to describe this wide range of provision are no longer officially used. Instead Supporting People Commissioning Bodies are encouraged to consider the purpose of individual sheltered schemes and the benefits and services available to residents to enable them to live independently.

Supporting People

Launched in April 2003, the programme aims to:

- Deliver quality of life and promote independence
- Ensure high quality, strategically planned, cost effective services that complement existing care services
- Plan and develop needs-led services
- Be a working partnership of local government, probation, health, voluntary sector organisations, housing associations, support agencies and service users.

Supporting People Administering Authorities

Manage Supporting People Grant contracts and undertake service reviews (see above). Usually run by the social services department in counties, and by either the housing department or by social services in London boroughs and other unitary authorities.

Supporting People Commissioning Body and Strategy Group

A partnership of local authority social services and housing, health and probation services which agrees the local Supporting People strategy (written by the Supporting People Core Strategy Group) and commissions services from support providers (primarily local authorities and housing associations).

Supporting People Five Year Strategies

Strategies which look at the current and projected housing and support needs and demands of vulnerable local people, including older people, and how the Supporting People Commissioning Body envisages these being met in future years.

Voids

Vacancies in a housing scheme. Typically measured by a loss of rental income for a period, and expressed as a percentage of the total income which could be received for the period. It may also be measured by the period until the property is re-let or the placement is filled.